GREAT WAR LITERATURE
STUDY GUIDE

Written by W Lawrance

on

FEMALE POETS
OF THE FIRST WORLD WAR

VOLUME ONE

Great War Literature Study Guide on Female Poets of the First World War - Volume One
Written by W Lawrance

Published by:
Great War Literature Publishing LLP
Darrington Lodge, Springfield Road, Camberley, Surrey GU15 1AB Great Britain
Web site: www.greatwarliterature.co.uk
E-Mail: editor@greatwarliterature.co.uk

First Edition published as paperback 2005

Produced in Great Britain

ISBN 1905378254 First Edition

Design and production by Great War Literature Publishing LLP
Typeset in Gill Sans and Trajan Pro

Great War Literature Study Guide on

Female Poets of the First World War - Volume One

CONTENTS

PREFACE

Great War Literature Study Guides' primary purpose is to provide in-depth analysis of First World War literature for GCSE and A-Level students.

There are plenty of other study guides available and while these make every effort to help with the analysis of war literature, they do so from a more general overview perspective.

Great War Literature Publishing have taken the positive decision to produce a more detailed and in-depth interpretation of selected works for students. We also actively promote the publication of our works in an electronic format via the Internet to give the broadest possible access.

Our publications can be used in isolation or in collaboration with other study guides. It is our aim to provide assistance with your understanding of First World War literature, not to provide the answers to specific questions. This approach provides the resources that allow the student the freedom to reach their own conclusions and express an independent viewpoint.

Great War Literature Study Guides can include elements such as biographical detail, historical significance, character assessment, synopsis of text, and analysis of poetry and themes.

The structure of Great War Literature Study Guides allows the reader to delve into a required section easily without the need to read from beginning to end. This is especially true of our e-Books.

The Great War Literature Study Guides have been thoroughly researched and are the result of over 20 years of experience of studying this particular genre.

Studying literature is not about being right or wrong, it is entirely a matter of opinion. The secret to success is developing the ability to form these opinions and to deliver them succinctly and reinforce them with quotes and clear references from the text.

Great War Literature Study Guides help to extend your knowledge of First World War literature and offer clear definitions and guidance to enhance your studying. Our clear and simple layouts make the guides easy to access and understand.

HOW TO STUDY POETRY

This might sound like quite a simple process, but in order to get the best out of reading and understanding poetry, here are a few tips:

1. Firstly, although this sounds obvious, read the poem through. You may not understand it the first time you read it, or you may think it is crystal clear - either way, it doesn't matter. Think about what you have read.

2. Then re-read the poem, but this time much more slowly, and, if possible, out load. Pay particular attention to any passages which you don't understand. Now make some notes on the parts which you do understand, and possible explanations, if you have any, for the more complicated passages.

3. Once you have written your notes, re-read the poem again. See if your perspective changes or whether you can understand the poem more clearly. At this point, I would suggest you start using the Study Guide to either re-inforce your opinions or help analyse the sections of poetry with which you are struggling.

4. We, deliberately, have not stressed too much importance on the literary form of the poems as this not a matter of opinion or conjecture. The form of a poem is able to be deduced from an understanding of literary terminology. Therefore, for your information, there is a Literary Glossary of terms available on our Web site at: www.greatwarliterature.co.uk/glossary.html

5. Some poets' work is easier to understand than others and, for this reason, it is essential that you have a thorough understanding of the poets themselves, which is why, in the Great War Literature Study Guides, the biographical detail always comes first.

INTRODUCTION

Within the vast number of books on the subject of the First World War and in particular, the literature of that period, the topic of the female writers is, all too often, neglected. Some poetry anthologies now include a token contribution from the female perspective - usually grouped under the chapter title of 'Home Front' or 'Non-combatant' poetry. Others choose to omit women's poetry altogether, leaving some readers to assume that female poetry is left out because it is unworthy or simply not very good - and in some cases this could certainly be true. Many women, however, wrote beautiful and moving poetry which described the effects the war had on them and the changing world in which they were learning to live.

During the First World War, the poetry which was popular and widely read was mainly of a nationalistic and patriotic variety, urging men to join the fighting. Some of this was written by men, such as Harold Begbie and Henry Newbolt and the government enthusiastically promoted the publication of this type of verse. The main female contributor to this genre was Jessie Pope, whose poetry is now frequently studied in schools and colleges, but her verse is, generally speaking, derided for both its tone and content. These poets, both male and female, portrayed war and death as glorious, injury was seen to be an honourable and necessary product of battle; and either of the above consequences was favourable to non-participation in the conflict.

After the war, when the number of casualties became more clear and the costs began to be counted, this sort of poet waned in popularity to be replaced by a more realistic wave of soldier-poets, many of whom also went on to write memoirs over the ensuing years. That is not to say that the soldier-poets were ignored during the war-years: Rupert Brooke's *1914 and Other Poems* was reprinted approximately every two months between May 1915 and the end of the war. Siegfried Sassoon's *The Old Huntsman* also sold well on its publication in May 1917. Much of the poetry written at the front came to have a special meaning for the public: *In Flanders Fields* by John McCrae, and *For the Fallen* by Laurence Binyon are two such examples. The end of the war marked a changing requirement in the production of poetry anthologies: soldiers were in, non-combatants were out.

One notable exception to this omission of the female influence, is Vera Brittain, whose poems and memoirs have remained popular and widely-read. One of the reasons behind this is the well-known history behind her writing. Vera Brittain lost her fiancé, her brother and two of her dearest friends, as well as serving as a VAD both in Britain and abroad during the war. This has led to a misrepresentation of women's writing from this period, where both Jessie Pope and Vera Brittain are seen as the main influences in the writing of women from this period: one representing 'the cause' and the other demonstrating 'the consequences'. This does scant justice to the contribution made by the female poets.

The tone and nature of women's writing is just as varied as that of their male counterparts. Many show a sense of anger and bitterness at the waste and futility of the war, which could rival that displayed by poets such as Siegfried Sassoon. Others focus on the effects which the war has had on them personally, while some give a more general viewpoint of the cost of the war to the nation as a whole.

The backgrounds of these women are as diverse as their poems: some were quite young when the war began, such as May Wedderburn Cannan. They were in love and frightened for the future. Their childhood and adolescent influences had a great bearing on their perception of the war. Eleanor Farjeon, for example, came from a happy, literary family and spent an idyllic and comfortable childhood. Shortly before the war, she had met Edward Thomas, and his death in April 1917 had a deep and profound effect on her life. Others, such as Katharine Tynan and Charlotte Mew were older and regarded the war from a different, more mature, perspective - Tynan, in particular, having two sons in the Army, feared for their lives and those of many other young men.

It should be remembered that not all 'home-front' or 'non-combatant' poetry was written by women. Among the male writers who, for various reasons, did not serve in the war are: Rudyard Kipling, G. K. Chesterton, Thomas Hardy and Wilfrid Wilson Gibson. This last poet's work shows such a depth of imagination, that his trench-life descriptions have caused many anthologists to assume that he was a 'soldier-poet', when in fact he never left Britain's shores during the war. His beautiful poem *Lament* demonstrates the reality of his feelings and shares a common theme with the writings of many of the female poets. Due to the misunderstanding regarding his status, however, readers are far more likely to find Gibson's work included in an anthology, than they are to find, for example, poems by Edith Nesbit or Margaret Postgate Cole.

In studying and praising the work of Owen, Sassoon, Rosenberg et al, we should not forget the valuable contribution made by the women, and other non-combatants, for that matter. A large number of the female poets served in the war; some in the Voluntary Aid Detachment or the Red Cross, or other branches of the services. Others worked in factories or on the land, doing the work of the men who had gone to fight. In some cases, they may have only been able to wait and weep but their poems provide an insight into that period of history and the far-reaching effects of war, death, fear and loss, as well as the changing role of women which the war brought about, the effects of which are still felt today.

MAY WEDDERBURN CANNAN

BIOGRAPHY

Although little is known of May's life after 1924, the detailed biography which follows, covering the years from her birth to her marriage, enables the reader to better understand the period before, during and immediately after the First World War, which shaped her poetry.

May Wedderburn Cannan was born in St Giles in Oxford on the 14th October 1893. Her twin sister Frances was the weaker of the two babies and, although neither was expected to survive, May clung on to life, while Frances did not. She died in December of that year. There was already one older sister, Margaret Dorothea (known by her second name), who had been born the previous November, and Joanna Maxwell was born in May 1896.

The family lived in Magdalen Gate House, which they rented from Magdalen College. May's father Charles Cannan was a tutor of Classics, who went on to become Dean of Trinity College, Oxford. He also sat on the Oxford City Council. In the late 1890s he became Secretary of the Oxford University Press and was instrumental in making it one of the greatest publishing houses in the world.

Her mother, Mary Wedderburn, came from an old and distinguished Scottish family. She spent much of her time during May's childhood tending to her own mother, who lived nearby, but needed a great deal of care since she was blind and widowed. As a result the girls spent a lot of time by themselves, overseen by a nanny, but essentially alone. They read and invented games, but May was short-sighted and clumsy and she felt isolated, as the middle child, since she was neither respected as the eldest or pitied as the baby.

In 1902 the girls stopped having a governess to tutor them at home and began attending Wychwood School. Here, May developed her love of English Literature, enjoying poetry, Shakespeare and Chaucer with equal relish. She also discovered an abiding passion for drama and acting which was to become a lifelong (and unfulfilled) ambition.

In 1908, the three girls, at their father's suggestion, published an anthology of children's verse entitled *The Tripled Crown*. They compiled it themselves, writing to various authors to gain consent to use their poems in the book. Later that year, Dorothea and May were sent away to school at Downe House, a newly-opened boarding school for girls. The school was, at that time, located in what had been Charles Darwin's house in the village of Downe in Kent.

May was unhappy at Downe - she missed Oxford and longed to pursue her acting. By 1910, Dorothea had left school, and May deeply resented having to return for a further three terms, especially as this would mean missing out on a visit to Oxford by Rudyard Kipling who was to stay with her family while his book *The History of England* was being printed at the Oxford University Press.

That winter, there was an outbreak of measles at Downe House and May became seriously ill. Her parents were summoned and, eventually, she was allowed to go home. Her heart had been affected by the pneumonia which she had also developed and she was to rest at home for three months. At this point it was decided, primarily by her father, that rather than returning to Downe, she should complete her education back at Wychwood.

At this stage, May became acquainted with Bevil Quiller-Couch, the son of her father's friend Sir Arthur Quiller-Couch. Bevil, who was attending Oxford, dined with the family regularly and often brought his rowing friends to visit too.

In 1911, May's mother became the first Commandant of one of Oxford's three Red Cross Voluntary Aid Detachments. When she turned 18, that October, May passed the necessary examinations and joined No 12 Detachment. In between training and lectures, these precious pre-war years continued pretty much as before: holidays in the Lake District and the Alps, house-parties, picnics, dances, writing and dreaming of a career on the stage. May also started helping out at the Oxford University Press, compiling indexes for various books.

Preparations for war began as early as 1913 when May, by now a Quartermaster in the VAD, was sent a list by the War Office, of equipment required to set up a hospital of sixty beds. She visited colleges and businesses in Oxford, asking for the use of various facilities when war broke out. The War Office also sent out inspectors to check that the various Detachments were being properly administered.

The summer of 1914 marked a change for May and her contemporaries. Although the parties and dances continued, there was always, in the background, a sense that their youth was being snatched away from them and that they were doing everything for the last time.

The family holidayed in Switzerland, but had to cut short their vacation when, on July 26th, they read a newspaper report which made it clear that war was imminent. May firmly believed that Britain should have declared war on Germany much earlier. She felt, in common with many others, that Germany's belief that Britain would remain neutral was what drove them on, and had Britain taken a firmer stance, Germany would have been halted. Rightly, or wrongly, this was a popularly held opinion at the time, borne largely out of the fact that many people firmly believed that Britain, with her strong Navy, was essentially invincible: that even the threat of Britain unleashing her military power would be sufficient to prevent a conflict.

Immediately war was declared, May's work started in earnest. She had to send out call-up telegrams to those of her Detachment who were outside of Oxford; organise collectors to visit those who had promised equipment or facilities during the previous summer; equip and furnish a hospital of 60 beds and arrange lodgings and food for the volunteers who were arriving to help. All of this was done with military precision and the task was completed within two days. May's friend Bevil Quiller-Couch was an army reservist and was mobilised on the 5th August, sailing for France on the 17th. By this time, he had fallen in love with May and had tried to get permission to visit her at Oxford prior to embarking for France. This was refused, so his marriage proposal which had been the reason behind his request, would have to wait. He wrote as often as he could to May.

Meanwhile, May and her nurses waited, unsure what to do next, or when the first casualties would arrive. There was great confusion, with many arms of the military closely guarding their own territory and equipment and a distinct lack of cooperation. Eventually, the order came through that hospitals such as May's were no longer required and that the volunteers would be used, as called for, in military hospitals. May was disappointed and angry. She decided to offer her hospital as a unit to the local military base, whose own facilities were incomplete. She walked to the base, which closely resembled a building site and her suggestion proved opportune since the commander of the base had been told that he was about to receive 60 wounded men, but he had nowhere to put them.

May was now unsure what to do - should she apply for a nursing position at another hospital, or stay and help her father at the Press. She decided on the latter. Most of the men at the Press had gone off to the war and May and her sisters took their places. Then at the end of August, came news of the British retreat from Mons, and suddenly May had to grow up. The Cannan family took in some refugees from Belgium who told them horrendous tales of the German invasion. Ninette, the youngest child, had nightmares and May would go to her in the night and hold her hand until she fell asleep again.

The Cannan sisters carried on working at the Press. Their work included printing some top secret papers for Naval Intelligence. Their father took a keen interest in the welfare of his print workers who had gone to the war - always ensuring that their families had enough money and were well taken care of. News was starting to filter through of casualties. Friends and acquaintances were listed as wounded or missing or dead. Bevil had survived his early encounters with the Germans and continued to write to May. Other friends, who had gone out to India with the regular army, now returned and embarked for France.

In April 1915 a family friend, Lucie Raleigh, invited May to join her at a Canteen in France for four weeks. May was enthusiastic to go: she wanted to share, even if only in a small way, in the work that was being done 'over there'. Her father agreed that she could go, so she and Lucie set off for Rouen. The work was hard and the hours were long - May frequently worked at night, feeding thousands of soldiers with tea and sandwiches, sometimes with less than two hours notice. She enjoyed her time in Rouen, but when her four weeks were over she returned home, reluctant to ask her father for an allowance which would enable her to stay.

At the end of May 1915, May was asked to return to her job in the VAD. She did so, on a part time basis, so as not to inconvenience her father too much. That summer was a great contrast with the 'golden' days of the previous year. The colleges at Oxford seemed empty; there were some young ladies in the women's colleges, but even they were restless and unsure where their future lay. Then came news of air raids on the coast, and there were warnings of raids in Oxford. Instead of parties and picnics, May's spare time - what little she had - was filled with war-work, although she still found time for reading poetry by Brooke, Grenfell, Sorley, Gibson and Sassoon.

There followed a cold winter. May felt that now people at home were finally beginning to understand that the war was going to last a very long time. The atmosphere had changed. In January 1916 came the first Military Service Act and, with it, conscription. May continued to write to Bevil and also wrote more and more poetry. She contemplated publishing a small volume or her work. In July 1916 came a letter from Bevil, informing her that he had been promoted and now had command of the 9th Battery, Royal Field Artillery.

The winter of 1917 was the worst winter of the war. It was particularly long and cold; food was becoming more scarce; civilians were depressed about the war. Things did not improve even when the Americans officially entered the war - their promises of help seemed so far in the future. May had now gathered quite a collection of poetry and she nervously approached Blackwells Publishers. They agreed to publish her anthology *In War Time*. When the printers at the Oxford University Press heard about this, they insisted that they be allowed to set up and print 'Miss May's' book. This first anthology achieved critical acclaim, but the tide was changing. That summer, Sassoon wrote his Declaration against the continuation of the war and people were becoming disenchanted with overly patriotic verse. May, however, remained convinced (like many others) that the cause for which they were fighting was just -

but the cost was becoming too great. Bevil wrote to her of the mud at Passchendaele and how he had used his revolver many times to shoot drowning horses. That September he was reported as wounded and hurriedly wrote to May to tell her that his wounds were not serious - in fact he had never even had to go out of the line.

Oxford was becoming busy again, Officer Cadets had filled the colleges and were being trained. Although there were no parties, as such, occasionally a young officer would be asked to dine with the Cannans. One of these young men, Staff Captain Nicholas Pullein-Thompson fell in love with Joanna, and asked her to marry him. She refused, but on his next leave, he asked again and this time she accepted. The whole family celebrated their engagement.

January 1918 saw Bevil on leave and he and May enjoyed an evening out in London. He wrote to May afterwards, telling her how much he had enjoyed seeing her again - although she remained unaware of the true depth of his feelings.

In March, the Germans launched their Spring Offensive and on the 28th of that month, May received a letter from Bevil saying that he had heard that Joanna's fiancé had been wounded, but not too seriously. Pullein-Thompson (known to the family as Nicki) was allowed home on sick leave and he and Joanna decided to marry in June. Their wedding day was perfect.

Joanna's marriage made May more contemplative about her own future. She longed to return to France, but it was deemed that she was not fit enough to go there with the Red Cross and the family finances would not allow her to return as an unpaid volunteer.

In the meantime, another romance was blossoming. Dorothea had decided to marry, in their mother's opinion, unwisely. The object of her affection was John Johnson, a relatively impoverished academic, who, having ruined his health during explorations in Egypt, now worked, temporarily with their father at the Press.

As luck would have it, their mother's objections were quashed when John was offered a permanent position at the Press. The couple were married on July 31st and May began to fear that she would never be able to return to France since she was the only one of the three sisters still working at the Press. Once again, however, fate took a hand and while May was enjoying a week's holiday in Cornwall, she received a letter offering her a job in a War Office Department in Paris. This letter said nothing of the position she would hold and suggested that if she was interested, she should journey to London, where she could be given more information. May, her curiosity aroused, wasted little time in fulfiling this request.

Following two interviews, May was accepted for the mysterious position and was told that she would leave for France two days later. She was, however, told very little about her new employment, other than the fact that it was 'in intelligence'. So, two days later, she embarked from Southampton for Le Havre, and eventually, Paris. She arrived there in the early hours of the morning, managing to get a lift in an empty American ambulance. Having found her way to her lodgings, she was given something to eat and gratefully fell into bed. The next morning, she met up with one of her co-workers, who told her the address of the office in which she would be working. For security reasons, May had not been given this information while she was still in England. On her way to her office, that first morning, there was an explosion in the street right in front of her. A horse was badly injured and a policeman appeared and shot it. Two wounded men were taken away in an ambulance and May was left standing in the street, somewhat bewildered. This was a rude introduction to the war in France.

Her job was in an office known as the 'British Mission' which was actually part of MI5. May initially worked in the 'Trade' department, dealing with smuggling and frontier infringements, but after only a few days, she was transferred to 'Espionage', which she found much more exciting. There were great restrictions to be contended with, however. Food was in even shorter supply in Paris than in Oxford; travelling was almost impossible and the German bombing campaigns made even a short walk out of doors into a dangerous pastime.

That autumn, May was promoted to Acting Head of the Women's Espionage Unit - she felt honoured, but also grateful because she had finally found a position in which she felt comfortable. Soon, the news of the war became more promising; the German guns withdrew and life became a little easier. Now, however, May faced another challenge - the influenza epidemic which would eventually engulf the whole of Europe was sweeping through Paris. There were no doctors or drugs - they were all being used to treat the soldiers. Many people died. Although May was infected, she recovered within a few days and was back at work.

Bevil's correspondence had continued and now he wrote that he intended to take his next leave in Paris, with her. On the morning of the 11th November, May was summoned into the Colonel's office, where she was ordered to take down a dictation of the Terms of the Armistice. May found this rather amusing, since her shorthand was more than a little rusty. She managed, however, and returned to her office where she made four copies of the document. Then she sat down and cried - it was all over.

A few days later, she attended a great parade in the streets, attended by the King, the Prince of Wales and all the European leaders and army chiefs. Initially, she was told to move away from the front of the crowd because, being in civilian clothes, she was presumed not to be a war worker. Undeterred, she went and stood with a group of Australian soldiers who looked after her and she watched proudly as the parade passed by.

At work, the office was being wound up, and May faced a decision - whether to apply for a job at the peace conference, or request demobilisation. Then, quite unexpectedly, Bevil arrived at her office - despite the fact that its location was a secret. As she walked down the stairs to meet him, May realised how deeply in love she was. Bevil had five days leave and they spent it together. They dined, walked and talked, rejoicing with the rest of Paris that the war was over and, for once, May enjoyed being young again. On the Saturday afternoon, Bevil collected her from work and as they walked by the River Seine, he asked her to marry him. When he returned to his unit, two days later, May went to the station with him, wearing his ring.

May, at Bevil's request, applied for demobilisation in order that she might be free to marry him as soon as he came home. By early December she was back in Oxford, looking forward to Bevil's return. He, meanwhile, was marching onwards into Germany and discovering that there were vast numbers of civilians prisoners of war, now released, whose homes had been destroyed by the fighting and who now had nothing. He wrote to May of how distressing this was to witness.

In January 1919, Bevil was granted leave and travelled at once to Oxford to see May. They spent a few days together there before going to Cornwall to see his family, who welcomed May warmly. This was a happy time of parties, dinners and celebration. They decided to fix their wedding date for the 3rd June. When Bevil returned to Germany, May decided to stay on in Cornwall for a few days before returning to Oxford, taking Bevil's sister with her.

On February 2nd Bevil wrote to May that he had caught a chill. This turned into influenza. On February 5th, May received word from Sir Arthur that Bevil now had pneumonia and was dangerously ill. May made enquiries with her former boss at the War Office to see if he could cut through some red tape and arrange for her to visit Bevil. He promised to do whatever he could. On the evening of the 7th, however, May received a telegram informing her that Bevil had died of pneumonia the previous day. The war, she felt, had completely changed her life: Bevil's death ended it.

May and Sir Arthur travelled to the War Office, but were refused permission to go to Germany for the funeral. Bevil was buried in Germany surrounded by friends, but May found it unforgivable that bureaucracy had prevented her from saying a final farewell. She returned to Cornwall with Sir Arthur and found that the whole town was in mourning for Bevil. She stayed with his family for some time and upon returning to Oxford, she toyed with the idea of going back to France to help with the refugees of whom Bevil had written. When she got home, however, she discovered that her father was ill, and she was reluctant to leave him again.

May, like many of her generation, became angry over the coming months, that some people who had stayed at home and made money during the war, were now able to dictate which of the returning soldiers would be employed. Men with years of enforced army experience were told that they were surplus to requirements, or that, having been out of normal employment for four years, they were no longer sufficiently qualified for positions they had previously held. For herself, May felt at a loss. She had continued to write verse, but knew she could not earn a living doing this and she, at 25, had no training or formal qualifications.

Then came a letter from the delegates (directors) of the Press, offering May her old job, together with a position assisting the new editor of the Oxford Magazine. May's father's health was deteriorating, but she was anxious to be busy and accepted this offer immediately.

During that summer, May began to socialise again, but only in a small way and always with people she had known before the war. She became re-acquainted with fellow poet Carola Oman, who had been nursing in France. They spent many hours together, walking, reading and discussing poetry. All of this provided some comfort for May, who found it difficult to sleep and hard to contemplate her future. In June she offered another selection of verse to Blackwells and they published them until the title *The Splendid Days*.

May was very lonely and threw herself into her work at the Press. She visited the Lake District with her parents one last time; and tried somewhat in vain, to join in the official Peace Celebrations that July. Always, however, she was reminded of everything that she had lost - not just her beloved Bevil, but all her hopes and her future. That autumn, she met T.E. Lawrence (Lawrence of Arabia). She found him restless and dissatisfied with the outcome of the war and the part he was seen to have played in it.

Early in November, May's father suffered a stroke and it soon became clear that he would not recover. He died on November 15th and was buried three days later. His colleagues from the Press lined the streets to say a final farewell. They remembered that he had taken great pains to ensure that every one of his staff who went to the war, and came back, was found employment. He had taken care of their families while they were away and they wished to pay their respects to him one last time.

May's mother decided that she could no longer bear to remain in their house, or for that matter, in Oxford. May was desolate. To her, Oxford had remained the one constant in her life. She begged her mother to reconsider, but it was not to be. They left early the following year. May initially went to Cornwall and stayed with Bevil's family and her mother stayed with one of May's sisters until they could decide where to live. By now, Bevil's beloved horse, Peggy, had been returned to his family by the War Office and May rode her a great deal, remembering happier days.

Initially, May's mother harboured ideas of settling in the West Country, and they stayed for a few weeks in Devon before moving on to Cornwall and eventually to the Scilly Isles. Eventually, however, she decided that she would prefer to live in London, so they found lodgings in Ebury Street, between Pimlico and Belgravia. May found employment at an office where the official history of the war was being written, and Bevil's letters and diaries proved invaluable, especially as he had served in the war, right from the beginning.

That winter, May and her mother went to stay in the South of France and then after Christmas, moved on to Switzerland and then Italy. It was in Florence and subsequently Rome, that May first began to be able to think about her future. Eventually, however, they were forced to leave Italy - there were Fascist uprisings, violence in the streets and strikes. They hurriedly packed and returned to England.

Back in London, May found employment at Kings College, looking after the welfare of 290 Ex-Service Students, who had been awarded grants to attend the college. This job, whilst enjoyable and rewarding, only lasted for one year, as most of the students were already in their third year and once they had graduated, May found herself, once again, looking for work. She was not alone - women all over the country, since the return of the men, now found themselves surplus to requirements. Before long, however, May found another job - this time at the Athenaeum Club, re-cataloguing the library and acting as assistant librarian. She was particularly nervous on her first day, since she was the first woman ever to work there.

Bevil's father came to visit her and the bond between them was as strong as ever. Rudyard Kipling visited in search of information for the War History of the Irish Guards which he was writing. May joined the Writers' Club which was a small club for women writers. On a visit to Cambridge in 1922, Bevil's father took May to visit Charles Hamilton Sorley's parents who welcomed her with such warmth that she was quite overcome.

In 1923, May's third volume of poetry *The House of Hope* was published and received good reviews. On a visit to Cornwall, Sir Arthur asked her if she had formed an attachment to another young man. May replied that a couple of old friends had expressed and interest in her, but that she felt that that part of her life was now over.

Early in 1924, she received two interesting letters: one from a young man, signing himself simply P.J.S. He wrote that he had admired her poetry and suggested that they should meet. The other letter came from her uncle, inviting her to join him as his secretary on a forthcoming trip to Canada and the USA. After much contemplation, May replied positively to both requests. She resigned from the Athenaeum and began to prepare for her trip across the Atlantic. In February, she met her young man who turned out to be Captain P J Slater, a solicitor. During the war he had served with the infantry until he was badly wounded. Once recovered, he had joined the RFC and served as a spotter in balloons, earning the Distinguished Flying Cross. By the end of June, May knew she was in love and within three months, the couple were married.

Little is known of what happened to May during the following years. Her husband was promoted to the rank of Brigadier during the Second World War, when he commanded an anti-aircraft brigade.

May died in 1973, leaving behind her a manuscript containing probably the best and most vivid descriptions of life before, during and immediately after the First World War, detailing its effects on a generation for whom life would never be the same again.

POETRY ANALYSIS

LAMPLIGHT

This poem tells of dreams and plans, built up by two young lovers, and the shattering of those hopes by war and death.

The first verse almost mocks the wisdom of youth, as there is a touch of irony in the first two lines. This couple made great plans, and being young and believing themselves invincible, they could see no obstacle to prevent their dreams from coming true. However, their wisdom has proved unfounded. The poem speaks of this couple, through their own hard work, building their own Empire. They do not seek for fame, but they want to serve their country.

All of this is reiterated in the second verse, where we now learn that while the man's desire was to see active military service for his country, the poet's choice is to become a nurse. In both of these verses, it is made clear that the poet is now alone, although she still believes she can see and hear her beloved, as she remembers their plans.

In the final verse, comes the revelation that none of their dreams will come true. They had never discussed him not coming back from the war, but this is the reality with which the poet is now faced. She only has her memories now and the crossed swords which denoted his active service have been replaced in her mind's eye, by a torn wooden cross which marks his grave.

This poem was written in December 1916, by which time many of May's friends had experienced the death of a loved-one. Although her closest friend, Bevil Quiller-Couch (to whom she would later become engaged) was safe, it would not have taken a great leap of the imagination for her to write this poem.

May felt, very strongly, right from the beginning of the war, that her generation would be changed beyond recognition by events over which they had no control. In the final few years before the war, which many have since described as 'golden', May's life had been quite pleasurable. There was, generally, a sense that youth gave one a certain invulnerability and that young people would in fact create a new and more exciting world, as they stepped out of the Victorian era into which they had been born. The war ended such hopes and this poem demonstrates the sense of anguish which affected many people at the time. The personal sacrifices made by so many reflect the overall loss suffered by an entire generation, who felt that they no longer had a future.

This would have been especially true at the end of 1916; a year which saw so many casualties in ultimately futile battles. The winter of 1916-17 was particularly long and harsh, which must have made the poet's outlook even more bleak.

Lamplight is similar in tone to *Perhaps* by Vera Brittain, which was addressed to her late fiancé Roland Leighton who died in December 1915. This poem lists the experiences which the poet believes she will either miss out on altogether, or which she will never enjoy again, because her beloved is dead.

Many of Vera Brittain's poems have this theme, such as *May Morning* (which was published in the Oxford Magazine), in which she wonders whether the survivors of the war will ever be able to recapture that carefree spirit which they used to have.

Lamplight beautifully evokes a sense of shattered youth and broken dreams, ended by a war in which many of its young participants had been keen to be involved. That blind enthusiasm made the end of their world all the harder to contemplate. The contrast, demonstrated in this poem, between the heady days of youth, and the cold bleak future, must have been almost unbearable.

'SINCE THEY HAVE DIED'

This short poem, written in February 1916, has a more optimistic tone than *Lamplight*. It is more a celebration of those who have died, and an urging to their survivors to remember the dead, not with sorrow, but with smiles.

The poet implies that the survivors owe their happiness to those who have died and that the best way to repay this gift is to perpetuate this emotion. By doing so, the dead will, themselves, find contentment.

This rose-coloured vision of the dead was commonly portrayed, especially in the first two years of the war, when many preferred to believe that their loved ones had died in a just cause and would rest in peace knowing that their survivors lived on in happiness. This made the whole idea of the gallant sacrifice seem more worthy.

Other poets who wrote in this tone included Rupert Brooke and John McCrae, who, in particular spoke of the dead in similar terms, as witnesses to the behaviour of their survivors. In *The Anxious Dead*, McCrae echoes the sentiments of *Since They Have Died*, in that his dead may finally turn contentedly to sleep, in the knowledge that they have not died in vain.

Later in the war, many poets would change their tone, allowing for the fact that slaughter on such as scale should not be seen as glorious at all. However, in the early days of the war, particularly before the Somme had claimed so many lives, May's opinion, demonstrated here, was not unusual.

One notable exception was Charles Hamilton Sorley, who in 1915 wrote *When You See Millions of the Mouthless Dead*. In this poem, the dead he describes are not laughing or contented. In fact they are unable to respond to the surviving mourners in any way for the simple reason that they are dead. This is a much harsher, and to those on the home-front, less palatable vision of death.

LOVE, 1916

This poem, written in August 1916, is essentially about how the emotion of love has changed and been transformed by the war. The date of the poem is worth noting, as by this stage, the full horror of the casualties from the beginning of the Battle of the Somme would have been realised.

In the poem, love is equated with other emotions, such as joy, the pursuit of power and fame, or the desire for peace. All of these are feelings which various people would have experienced. For example, before the war, May, as a young innocent girl, would have looked upon love as a joyous emotion - at once exciting and fulfiling and bringing happiness. On the other hand, many, including those who had sought war had a passion for power as intense as any conventional love affair. Equal to this was the deep desire which everyone felt for peace.

The poet asserts that, upon summoning love, in any of these forms, she has discovered that it bears another name: sacrifice. The demands which have been placed on all of her generation far outweigh their previously powerful emotions. Joy, power, fame and the hope for peace have all been erased and replaced by the sacrifice of love and youth.

She could also have been implying here that to sacrifice a loved-one demonstrates the ultimate love of someone who will relinquish their own happiness for the sake of others. Either way, her previously held convictions on that emotion have been altered beyond recognition.

This is a sad poem which evokes a feeling of loneliness: she is looking for love, calling out for it even, only to discover that it no longer exists in any form known to her, or her generation. It signifies the fact that everything has changed - nothing is as it used to be.

ROUEN

26th April - 25th May 1915

This poem offers a very evocative description of May's time at Rouen, working in a Canteen at the Rail Head. In it, she conveys the atmosphere both in and around her workplace; sights, sounds and smells are brought to life.

May wrote this poem in the form of questions about remembrances of a time which, for her, was very happy and fulfiling. For her this was a great adventure, as she had longed to be in France and taste the reality of war first hand.

Throughout the poem she describes various aspects of daily life in the canteen, from the sunrises she witnesses at the end of her shift (May worked mainly during the night), to the strange voices of the Indian soldiers who served during the war. One phrase which often provokes questions in this poem relates to tatties and why they would make a clicking sound. A tattie is the name given, in India, to a screen of grass fibres which was hung at a door or window opening. In India, this screen would have been kept wet to moisten and cool the air. We may, therefore, suppose that screens similar to these were used in the canteens. Either they would be caught in the wind, or as people passed through them, they would bang on the door frame, thus making the clicking sound referred to. May might have heard the Indian soldiers refer to the screens as tatties, or she might have already known about them, since she had some old Oxford friends who had gone out to India with the regular army before the First World War, and she may have picked up the word from them.

She describes the contrast between the still sleeping town, and the hoards of hungry soldiers, laughing over their coffee and sandwiches before going on towards the front. When the soldiers finish and their trains are ready to depart, they are called to attention and sing *God Save the King*.

Suddenly the canteen is quiet again, all the men have left, and although dawn approaches promising a new beginning, she perceives that the men are travelling to and from darkness. However, everything carries on: there is another shift of workers to hand over to; another train full of soldiers in need of refreshment and a smile. Having completed her own shift, May is now free to enjoy the cool calmness of the morning and to sleep.

In the final two verses, the tone of the poem changes, May is no longer asking whether others share her remembrances - she is telling us that *she does* remember. She is looking back to her time in Rouen and her adventures there, with an almost romantic air. Her pride in the soldiers is there in the final verse, in that her most abiding memory is of the trains carrying them towards the war. May perceived that the men were fighting gallantly for a worthy cause, and held the soldiers in high esteem.

The fondness of May's memories of that time is apparent in this poem. When she returned to Oxford after her month in Rouen, she felt that she would give almost anything to be able to return to France. She had a profound sense of belonging there: that she was, even only in a small way, doing 'her bit' for the war effort, and in doing so, she felt fulfiled.

MARGARET POSTGATE COLE

BIOGRAPHY

Born in Cambridge on May 6th 1893, Margaret Isabel Postgate was the daughter of John Percival Postgate and Edith Allen. She was the eldest of three children. Raymond and Percival, her brothers, were three and six years younger than her, respectively. The family lived in a house called Sunnyside in Church Road, Stapleford, in Cambridgeshire. Her father had been Professor of Latin at the University of Liverpool. Margaret was educated at Roedean School, overlooking the Sussex Downs. She then returned to Cambridge and attended Girton College.

Although she had been raised in the Anglican faith, while Margaret was at University, she began questioning her religious beliefs. She became a socialist, a feminist and a pacifist and upon the outbreak of the First World War she became actively involved in the peace movement. She and her brother, Raymond, campaigned against conscription and Raymond was imprisoned as a conscientious objector.

Margaret met George Douglas Cole, another conscientious objector, and the two were married in 1918, working together at the Fabian Research Department. After the war, the couple moved to Oxford where Margaret taught evening classes. Between 1923 and 1946, Margaret and George wrote many crime novels featuring Superintendent Henry Wilson of Scotland Yard.

During the 1930s, following the destruction of the Socialist movement in Germany, Margaret lost her belief in pacifism and supported Britain's role in the Second World War. She died in 1980.

POETRY ANALYSIS

THE FALLING LEAVES (NOVEMBER 1915)

This short poem compares the falling leaves of autumn with the fallen soldiers in Flanders.

A picture is conjured of a young woman riding down a lane on a late autumn day, witnessing the falling of leaves, despite there being no wind. This scene is compared with the silence of a heavy snowfall, rather than the noise and bluster usually associated with a windy autumn day. This makes the rider think of the brave young men who are dying at the Front, not through old-age or illness, but because of war. Like the leaves, their dying youth and beauty reminds her of snowflakes which must by now be falling at the Front.

This poem is beautiful and yet without hope. The use of autumn leaves and snowflakes are symbolic of death. When the leaves reach the ground, they are dead because they are starved of nutrients; the snowflakes must also eventually "die" because they melt. This represents the dying men at the Front and it could be interpreted that the soldiers die because they too are starved. In their case, however, they are deprived of hope, of a future, of the warmth and love of home and family. One feels that their lives are wasted, just like the leaves. The dead soldiers will also eventually "melt" into the soil, and disappear just as the snowflakes do.

The poet perceives the soldiers as brave and comments on the vast number of men who will perish, which again relates back to the leaves and the snowflakes. This ability to recognise that the quantity of dead will be multitudinous, demonstrates great foresight on the part of the writer, bearing in mind that this poem was written fairly early in the War.

There is no sense of glory or patriotism here, merely sadness at the passing of so many, for so little. These men have not been allowed to grow old, or even become ill, but have been struck down in their prime, at their most beautiful, their deaths being as inevitable as the falling of the leaves.

PRAEMATURI

This poem contrasts the feelings of old people, whose friends die, with those of the young, who must face a long future alone.

In the first verse the poet describes her imagined sense of how an older person might feel upon the death of a contemporary. Although they might feel sad, they have many years of memories, and, being old, will, in theory not have too long to dwell on the prospect of being alone.

The second stanza deals with the effects of the death of young people on their friends. These people who have had precious little time to experience the joys of life, are now torn apart, with no hope for the future, but many years to rue their youth.

This is a sad poem which reflects on the feelings of those who have lost someone in the war: not the mother losing a son, but the girl losing a friend or lover. The contrast is drawn between old and young: the old have lived their lives, had their opportunities, and now have happy memories upon which to reflect.

The young, on the other hand, have had no chance to even create happy memories and must spend many years considering what might have been. Youth is portrayed as a curse, since the old people are shown as contentedly looking forward to rejoining their departed friends. The young people wish to be dead, and join those they have lost, but are doomed to live for many years, an empty and unfulfilling life.

This poem paints a depressing picture of a generation torn apart, whose capacity to enjoy life to the full has been snatched away by the war and the deaths of so many young men. These deaths have come suddenly, not as the result of old-age or illness, not naturally with the passing of time, but through violence.

Despite the fact that she is female, and one assumes she is writing from a woman's perspective, the author compares the survivors to old *men*, making use of irony. This could be because she feels that when she becomes old, there will be no old men, because they have all been killed in their youth and none will, therefore, survive to old age.

In the hopeless world created by this poem, such an attitude is quite easy to understand: as the casualty lists grew longer, it must have seemed that all hope for the future was dying too.

THE VETERAN (MAY 1916)

This poem relates an episode in which a group of (presumably) young ladies, come upon a blinded soldier sitting in the sunshine. They are joined by some young soldiers, fresh from the pub, who ask the blind man's advice. He tells them his stories, which seem to fall on deaf ears. After the soldiers have gone, the blind man becomes aware that someone else is still present and openly pities the young soldiers' inexperience. He sits, his eyes turning towards where he believes his companions have gone, until one of the young ladies asks him how old he is and he reveals that he is just nineteen years of age.

The irony in the title of this poem should not go unnoticed. This man is considered a veteran when, having only just turned nineteen, he was not old enough to have been serving in the first place. (The age for going overseas on active service during the First World War was nineteen, although many young men lied about their age, particularly in the early years of the war, fearing that if they waited they would "miss out").

For the first two verses, the reader is unaware of the man's age, and one assumes that he is older, in view of the fact that the other soldiers are referred to as being young and are asking advice from this more experienced man. These young soldiers are complacent and pay little heed to what the blind man tells them. He does not berate them, but pities their innocence which he knows will soon be lost. It is also easier for the reader to make the assumption that the man must be older: after all who wants to believe that someone so young could have lost his sight? This lulls the reader into a false sense of security.

The blind man is portrayed as lonely, while the others are all in groups, which is reminiscent of Wilfred Owen's poem *Disabled,* in which a maimed soldier sits alone, abandoned by his friends who fear the sight of him, and rejected by women, in favour of the men who are still whole. In *The Veteran*, the young soldiers, although keen for the blind man's advice, do not remain long, possibly because his plight reminds them of what might await them in France.

The young ladies remain a little longer, and eventually one of them asks how old the blind man is - this shows that his extreme youth is not obvious and maybe, like Owen's maimed soldier in *Disabled*, he has grown old before his time.

This poem does not glorify war, nor is there a hint of patriotism. Like much of Margaret Postgate Cole's poetry one is left with an acute feeling of sadness: youth is being wasted and the expectations of a nation, which are being placed on these young men, are too great for their generation to bear.

NANCY CUNARD

BIOGRAPHY

Nancy Cunard was born on 10th March 1896 at her family's home, Nevill Holt in Leicestershire. She was the only child of Sir Bache Cunard, a Baronet and heir to the Cunard Shipping line. Although a British subject, he was born in New York in 1852. Nancy's mother, an heiress in her own right, had been born Maud Alice Burke in San Francisco in 1872. The couple married when Maud was just twenty years old and she and Sir Bache - who was twice her age - moved into the Cunard family residence.

Maud's exuberant and youthful personality ensured that Nevill Holt became a centre of social activity. Nancy's arrival cause little change, and the young child was brought up mainly by servants and governesses. When her parents were present, there were many parties, where Nancy was allowed to stay up late and mix with prominent figures from the worlds of literature, art, music and politics.

In 1910, when Nancy was fourteen, her parents separated and mother and daughter moved to London. Nancy's mother, by now better known as 'Emerald', continued to live up to her reputation of leading socialite, while Nancy was sent to private schools in London, Paris and Germany.

It was during 1914, while attending school in Paris, that Nancy became involved with a group known as the 'Corrupt Coterie' - an unconventional collection of writers and artists, including Osbert

Sitwell, Ezra Pound, Augustus John and Diana Manners. This group would be found, most evenings, sitting in Parisian cafés, discussing poetry and politics. Nancy's involvement was acknowledged as a rebellion against her mother - and the traditions of debutantes and marriage. Nancy and her particular friend, Iris Tree, were reputedly 'truly bad girls' - they rented a studio room, Nancy wore men's clothes and they indulged in unusually promiscuous behaviour, liberally fuelled by excessive amounts of alcohol. Other participants in the group included the younger members of many leading families of the British aristocracy, such as the Grenfells, Tennants and Asquiths - most of whom would die in the trenches of the First World War - the 'Coterie' dying with them.

Given Nancy's behaviour at this time, it came as quite a shock to both her family and friends, when in 1916, she announced her engagement to Sydney Fairbairn, an army officer of short acquaintance. Fairbairn was regarded as socially acceptable, but dull and most unlike Nancy's other male acquaintances. Nobody was particularly surprised when their marriage ended in separation after only twenty months, although they did not officially divorce until 1925.

Nancy almost immediately became intimately involved with another serving army officer: Peter Broughton-Adderley. It has been claimed that she never fully recovered from his death, less than one month before Armistice Day.

Returning to Paris in 1920, Nancy became increasingly dependant on alcohol and also started to experiment with various recreational drugs. She became involved in Dadaism, Modernism and Surrealism and, although not an active member of a political organisation, she took a keen interest in Communism. She embarked on a series of affairs with, amongst others, novelist Michael Arlen, writer Aldous Huxley and historian and poet Louis Aragon. When this last relationship ended, it is alleged that Aragon attempted suicide.

In 1927, Nancy founded The Hours Press at a farmhouse in Reanville, outside Paris. Here she set about publishing works by authors who, for various reasons, had struggled to gain recognition elsewhere. These included Ezra Pound, Robert Graves and Richard Aldington.

Always one to flout convention, Nancy's next relationship would shock many, including her mother. She had earlier met the black American jazz musician, Henry Crowder, and in 1928 he moved into the farmhouse. When 'Emerald' heard of Nancy's newest lover, she disinherited her daughter and the two women did not speak for many years.

Nancy's involvement with Crowder fuelled her interest in the Civil Rights movement in America, although her behaviour continued to cause controversy. She painted her face white, her lips dark red and generously applied rouge (many say she did this with a rabbit's foot); she wore ivory and bakelite bangles on both arms, from wrist to elbow. She and Crowder certainly made an unusually striking couple. In addition to this, theirs was a turbulent relationship - the calm, placid Crowder often falling victim to Nancy's violent, alcohol-driven temper.

In customary style, once Nancy had tired of Crowder, she moved on - to Spain. She lived there through most of the 1930's, working as a freelance writer during the Spanish Civil War. For some of this time, she lived with the poet Pablo Neruda, whose poems she translated.

She spent the Second World War in London, returning to the Reanville farmhouse upon its conclusion. There, she discovered that most of her possessions had been destroyed or stolen - whether by the Nazi's or the locals is unclear. She never lived there again.

Over the ensuing years, she drifted around in an alcoholic haze, on at least one occasion appearing in a magistrate's court on a charge of disorderly conduct. Even here, however, her temper got the better of her and she removed her shoes and hurled them at the presiding official.

By 1960 her wild lifestyle had started to really catch up with her and she was committed to Holloway Sanatorium due to her mental instability. Her cousin Victor Cunard secured her release and took care of her until she could arrange to return to France. Once there, however, her health and mental stability continued to deteriorate; she alienated all of her friends, who had always tried to be understanding of her behaviour. On 15th March 1965, the Parisian police found her walking the streets in a confused state. They took her to the Cochin charity hospital, where she died two days later, aged sixty-nine.

One observer reportedly said that, despite the outrageous behaviour, unusual clothes and make-up, if you looked into her blue eyes you would find a visible, deep sadness. This remained with her, despite all the supposed advantages of her birth, from her early wild-child days, through her hedonistic, yet unfulfilling love-affairs, to her ultimately sad and lonely death.

POETRY ANALYSIS

ZEPPELINS

This poem describes the fear, almost to the point of madness, which results from a Zeppelin raid. These raids became quite common - at a rate of roughly two per month - from early 1915. During that year, the Germans launched many successful raids on London, causing loss of life and destruction of property on a scale never witnessed before. Zeppelin raids tailed off slightly from 1916 onwards, but they had done more damage than merely the physical: the psychological effect on civilians was their greatest achievement and Nancy Cunard's poem reflects this.

Initially, she describes the people as climbing to escape from the approaching Zeppelin. This could be because they are, literally, running uphill; alternatively this word may be used to represent a greater sense of fear and panic - it is more difficult to have to climb up away from something than merely to run.

It would seem that the people have gone mad with fear, yet they have also gained a certain strength and through this, a wish to avenge the deaths of so many in the trenches. Therefore, they initially manage to overcome their fear with thoughts of vengeance and killing. Death, in the form of the Zeppelin, pursues them, appearing almost stately, as it hovers above them, waiting to unleash its bombs. The explosions caused sound like this giant representative of death is stamping its feet.

The fires which follow destroy the rows of houses. 'Serried' means closed ranks and while here it refers to the houses, it is more usually used in reference to troops. This provides an interesting metaphor between the homes of these frightened civilians and the soldiers serving in the trenches. The area most affected is the poorer district, which is also referred to as sad. This may be a reference to the fact that Cunard might have automatically assumed that poor people would be sad, it could also mean that the people in poorer areas seemed to suffer more than most - especially at that time. Although many upper and middle class families had relatives serving at the front, sheer numbers alone dictated that most of the losses would occur in the working class areas. So, in addition to their usual fears and worries, they are now faced with the additional threat of the loss of a loved-one, and now their own destruction.

Both death and the people are portrayed as mad. However, death is perceived as superior because its stamping feet - the bombs - are said to be proud. This makes death more powerful and controlling over the panicking crowds, many of whom die or hide away in their fear. The blackness of the night would have been enhanced by the blackout which the authorities had put into operation in an attempt to thwart the Zeppelin raids. One side-effect of this, however, was that the bombings became more indiscriminate - so the night may well have appeared frenzied, since the people would not know when or where the bombs would fall - and to a certain extent, neither would the bombers themselves - it has been estimated that only about 10% of the bombs dropped by the Zeppelins actually hit their intended target.

Despite their attempts to hide, or run away, death continues to pursue the people. However, Cunard now gives death an ecclesiastical - almost innocent - air, in that the Zeppelin's covering, rather than being the ragged fabric of the first verse, is now a gown, like those worn by choirboys. It seems to be streaked, like the people's faces - the shadows on both creating an almost mirrored expression - one fearsome, one frightened.

Finally, however, daylight returns and fear abates. There is a contrast here between light and dark, the mad fear of death and the mocking arrogance of having escaped and survived.

This poem illustrates the power of death and how the fear of it can easily control ones actions. Although the symbol of death in this poem is the Zeppelin, this could be seen as representative of all the death and destruction surrounding everyone at that time, from which there was no escape. This is particularly so, given Cunard's reference to the destroyed houses appearing to be like rows of soldiers. There is an element of relentless fear in this poem, which over the course of time has led to madness. Again, this could be an allusion to the soldiers who, having eventually become exhausted by the constant fear, noise and destruction of the trenches, exhibited outward signs of terror, almost like madness - better known eventually as shellshock. The overpowering dread of the people is contrasted with the calm, controlling Zeppelin which wreaks havoc on so many, just like the war has done.

Other poets described Zeppelin raids, using them to represent the feelings of those on the home-front. For example, Laurence Binyon's *The Zeppelin* which describes the initial fear of the civilians, turning into a sense of pride and thanksgiving that they are able to share in the danger being experienced by those at the front, and by doing so, they gain a greater understanding of the war.

Cunard's poem has a different focus - concentrating more on fear, tinged with an element of madness. This is partly because she is trying to point out that death comes unseen, in whatever form it strikes - as a bomb from a Zeppelin, or a telegram delivered to the door. It also has something to do with the underlying message of her poem: that any group of people who live in constant fear of anything, will eventually start to lose their sense proportion and control over their own lives and that while daylight may bring relief from these terrors, that is only temporary: the darkness of one's fear and the unknown is blacker than ever.

ELEANOR FARJEON

BIOGRAPHY

Eleanor Farjeon was, it could be argued, destined to become a writer. Her family background and childhood ensured that books and reading had a great influence on her early life. Her father, Benjamin Leopold Farjeon, was a born story-teller of Jewish descendency, who adored books and reading and initially found employment as a compositor on the journal *The Nonconformist*. He yearned, however, to become an author and at the age of 16, following a disagreement with his father, he emigrated to Australia to seek his fortune in the gold fields. Seven years later, he moved on to New Zealand, settling in Dunedin. Here, with Julius Vogel, he founded and managed the *Otago Times*. He also began writing plays and stories. One such was a Christmas story which he dedicated to his literary hero, Charles Dickens. In 1866 Dickens sent him a letter of thanks and acknowledgement, and upon receipt of this Benjamin decided to give up his successful life in New Zealand and return to England to follow his ambition of becoming a writer.

Eleanor's mother also came from a family where the written word was of great importance: her father was the American actor Joseph Jefferson. Following her mother's death when she was seven years old, Margaret Jefferson travelled with her father to Australia and New Zealand. Here they met Benjamin Farjeon, but although they saw a fair amount of the young English writer, they lost contact with him when they left Dunedin for London. They returned to New York in 1866, when Margaret was 13 years old. By now Margaret had dropped her childhood nickname of 'Tiddie' and preferred to be called 'Maggie'. In 1875 when Maggie was 22 years old, she once again went travelling with her father - this time to England, where he looked forward to renewing his acquaintance with his old friend Benjamin Farjeon. Maggie had a mental image of this now famous and critically acclaimed author as a white haired old gentleman, but she eagerly anticipating meeting her father's friend whose books she had read and greatly admired.

When Maggie and Benjamin met, she was surprised by his youth (although he was fifteen years her senior), and he was immediately captivated by her beauty and poise. The attraction between them was obvious and they began to see a great deal of each other. Early in 1877, Benjamin sought Joseph's permission to ask for Maggie's hand in marriage. She quickly accepted and the couple were married on 6th June of that year in London, and decided that they would live in America. Their first child, Harry, was born exactly eleven months after their marriage, but Benjamin was finding it difficult to settle in America, so when Harry was four months old, the young family sailed for England and found lodgings in Buckingham Street, near Charing Cross in London.

Among their frequent and numerous visitors here were Maurice and Georgie Barrymore, whose children, Lionel, Ethel and John would go on to become renowned actors. On March 20th 1880 Charlie Farjeon was born. He inherited his maternal grandfather's pulmonary problems and was very ill as an infant.

Eleanor, who was known to her family as 'Nellie' was born within a year, on 13th February 1881. That summer, despite the joy of the arrival of a longed-for daughter, Maggie faced the greatest of all sorrows, when young Charlie died at the age of 16 months.

Harry and Nellie shared their nursery with a young nurse, Julia whose time at Buckingham Street only lasted until Maggie's discovery of bruises on Harry's arms, which he explained by revealing that Julia would pinch him if he misbehaved. Julia left the house the very next day and was replaced by Fanny Dodd who had a great sense of humour and loved the children under her charge as though they were her own.

The family moved to a larger house in Adelaide Road, Chalk Farm, North London where there was a garden in which Harry and Nellie could keep rabbits. This move was necessitated by the arrival in June 1883 of Joe Jefferson Farjeon. Not long after his birth, however, Maggie became seriously ill and a specialist informed Benjamin that there was every possibility that his young wife would not survive. Benjamin refused to accept this and through sheer willpower and determination, he pulled Maggie through her illness and, in fact, she lived for another fifty years, although her health would always remain a concern.

Harry and Nellie were extremely close as children, enjoying trips to the zoo and holidays in Margate. In 1886, the family moved further up Adelaide Road to a larger house in order to make room for the final Farjeon: Herbert (Bertie) who was born in March of the following year.

By now, Eleanor had begun 'writing' - these early pieces had to be dictated to her father, but throughout her childhood she always showed her literary efforts to Benjamin. She was too embarrassed to remain in the room with him while he read her manuscripts and would run away to the nursery to await his verdict. He advised her on every aspect of writing, from language and grammar to preparing her copy for printers although this was obviously a dim and distant dream at this early stage of her life. Benjamin always took her writing seriously, he was never patronising and always encouraged her: particularly good pieces were copied out into his 'special' book, which he always treasured.

The four Farjeon children spent a happy childhood, inventing nursery games, listening to their father read aloud, singing and dancing while their mother accompanied them on the guitar or piano. Harry was the principal inventor of games and activities and ruled the nursery with a firm, but fair, hand. Nellie was a shy child, wholly absorbed in her writing and exceptionally attached to her older brother. Shortly before Nellie's eighth birthday, it was discovered that she had extremely poor eyesight. She was taken to an oculist, who gave her a pair of spectacles, but warned against the over-straining of her eyes. Nellie was amazed to discover, upon first wearing her spectacles, that there were patterns on the wallpaper. Her father, concerned for her eyes, yet equally keen that her interest in reading should not suffer, scoured bookshops to find books with larger print, and if this proved impossible he read to her himself, so that at no time should she feel that she was missing out.

Nellie was educated entirely at home by a nursery governess, but also by reading the many books which surrounded her. Her brothers all attended day schools, but Nellie spent many hours, when she was not studying, in the little book room at the top of the house. Here, among the worn and dusty volumes, she discovered other worlds. She also developed a keen interest in nature and art and wrote poems about both. Nellie showed little interest in formal education until the arrival of Miss Lily Newman as her governess. Miss Newman managed to capture Nellie's interest and encouraged her to learn more so that she would be able to write with a greater depth of knowledge and understanding.

As they grew up, the children began to accompany their parents to the theatre - an atmosphere which captivated Nellie from her very first visit. Due to their parents' connections, they usually went backstage after performances to meet the cast. Nellie's childhood was spent in the company of many late Victorian 'greats' of the theatre, such as Henry Irving, Ellen Terry and Sarah Bernhardt.

When Nellie was 13 years old, Harry began attending the Royal Academy of Music. Initially Nellie was devastated at the departure of her beloved brother, but his composing of music opened other doors for her as she began to write lyrics for him, many of which were performed in public over the following years.

In 1898, the family moved to 11 Lancaster Road, where Nellie was given the largest bedroom so that she could have her desk and typewriter always available. She was, however, suffering from a crisis of confidence and found it difficult to write. At about this time, Benjamin Farjeon became ill. He continued to write, but his books no longer sold in sufficient quantities to meet the family's financial requirements. In 1903, his health became worse, but the children, unaware of the serious nature of his illness, carried on as normal. There was a long-awaited visit by some of Maggie's American relatives to prepare for. On 22nd July, Benjamin seemed to improve: his pain had diminished and the doctors seemed more positive. Nellie did not visit her father's room on that day, partly because she was relieved at his improvement and wanted him to get as much rest as possible, and also because she was kept busy entertaining the newly arrived American relatives. Late that night, Nellie was roused by her mother and was told to wake Harry but not the younger boys or their guests. Her father's condition had, once again, deteriorated.

Nellie, Harry and their mother sat together in Nellie's bedroom waiting for the inevitable knock on the door which informed them that Benjamin had died. The family grieved deeply for him - Maggie was inconsolable, while the children attempted to oversee the arrangements and deal with all the visitors and well-wishers who called at the house.

After Benjamin's funeral it soon became clear that the family could no longer maintain their previous lifestyle. Smaller accommodation was found at 137 Fellows Road; money was sent from America to help with immediate expenses and books and furniture had to be sold to raise funds.

Harry was appointed Professor of Harmony at the Royal Academy of Music and became the sole wage-earner in the household. Joe and Bertie also sought work, while Nellie completed her father's unfinished manuscripts. Bertie went on to became a lyricist and writer, while Joe wrote thrillers as both novels and plays.

As the years passed, the four Farjeons would always remain close: Eleanor and Herbert collaborated in the writing of a light opera entitled *An Elephant in Arcady*. Eleanor continued to write stories and poems, many of which reflected her ideals of love, loyalty and romance - sentiments which she always tempered with practicality.

In November 1912, Eleanor was introduced to Edward Thomas, who shared her love of nature and books. They were both shy, but almost immediately a close friendship began. For Eleanor, this friendship soon blossomed into love but she remained silent about her feelings for Edward: he was happily married and devoted to his wife, Helen, and their three children. Eleanor feared that if she revealed her love for Edward, he would feel duty-bound to end their friendship and besides, it was not in her nature to wilfully hurt another person. She often visited Edward's family home in Hampshire and encouraged him to write. In January 1915 she began typing out his poems in preparation for sending them off to potential publishers.

On 15th July 1915, Edward enlisted in the Artists Rifles, following many months of indecision. Eleanor sensed that reaching this decision made him much happier and he seemed less tormented than he had of late. Following his training, Edward received his orders to embark for France. Eleanor spent the 8th and 9th of January 1917 with Helen and Edward, before bidding him a final farewell. He left for France two days later. This was a very emotional and poignant time for Eleanor who knew, beyond doubt, that she was acting properly, yet deeply regretted that Edward was leaving, unaware of her true feelings for him.

On 9th April 1917 Edward Thomas was killed in a shell-blast and this news reached Eleanor at Fellows Road. She was devastated, but responded immediately to Helen's request that she should join the Thomas family at their home. Helen's original idea in suggesting this had been that Eleanor might find solace by spending time with Edward's family. However, Helen's own grief was quite overwhelming and Eleanor found herself in the position of comforter to Edward's wife. Despite her own aching loss, Eleanor also managed to offer practical assistance, helping with shopping, preparing meals and taking care of the children.

Her own grief, she found, seemed insignificant when compared with Helen's and Eleanor came to realise that the scenes of bereavement which she was now witnessing were being repeated in homes all across the country and indeed, around the world.

After staying with Helen for two weeks, Eleanor returned to Fellows Road and the comfort of her own dear family. She made no secret, in later years, of the fact that Edward Thomas had been her greatest love, but this love remained unrequited and unconfessed due to Edward's undying love and devotion to Helen and Eleanor's respect for that.

After the war, Eleanor once again found herself involved with a married man. The gentleman in question was an English teacher named George Earle. Once it became clear that his marriage was over, Eleanor felt free to declare her feelings for him. They never married, but shared a close and lasting relationship until his death in November 1949. Earle (who was nicknamed 'Pod') had a passion for Keats and carpentry. He respected Eleanor's intellectual abilities, and her devotion to him never diminished, although in later years she would confess that her feelings towards him had always been more maternal than romantic. During her time with Earle, Eleanor also spent twelve years nursing her mother through a painful illness, before her eventual death in 1933.

Following Earle's death in 1949 Eleanor, now aged 68, threw herself into the production of her play *The Silver Curlew* which was being performed as a Christmas entertainment by The Arts Theatre. While at rehearsals, she came across an actor she had met ten years earlier: Denys Blakelock. He was prone to depression and self-doubt and Eleanor eased his fears in any way she could. She solved practical problems such as arranging for a new electric heater to be delivered to his dressing room, when the old one broke down, and supplied coffee and sandwiches for lunch - a meal she knew he often neglected. In addition, she provided great moral support and boosted Blakelock's flagging confidence.

When the play finished, in January 1950, Blakelock went away for a few weeks, but found a letter from Eleanor waiting for him when he arrived at his destination. This was the beginning of a close friendship which would last fifteen years, ending only with Eleanor's death.

By the time Eleanor began her friendship with Blakelock, two of her beloved brothers were dead. Bertie, the youngest, died first, in 1945, followed in 1948 by Harry.

Eleanor taught Blakelock to appreciate poetry and, to a certain extent, music and through him, she recaptured an element of her youth - namely going backstage after a performance to meet the actors. On August 22nd 1951, Eleanor was received into the Catholic church in a baptism held at St James's in Spanish Place in London.

In 1955, Eleanor published her story *The Little Bookroom* which won the first ever Hans Andersen Award for 'continued distinguished contribution to children's literature' and the Carnegie Medal for 'the best children's book of the year'. Eleanor's books were often aimed at children and their inspiration was her own idyllic childhood and the nursery games invented by Harry. She chose, however, to rarely talk about her work, never analysing it, but accepting its creation as the next step in the make-believe games. In the same year as this literary triumph, Eleanor lost the last remaining link with her childhood: Joe died. Her faith in God and friendship with Denys Blakelock helped her through this difficult time, as in later years, she would draw on these comforts through her own final illness.

She remained active and continued writing until she was 84 when illness and the failure of her eyesight forced her to give up. One of the last things she wrote was the foreword to a new collection of Edward Thomas's poems. Eleanor Farjeon died on 5th June 1965. Among her many literary achievements, as well as writing countless stories and poems for adults and children, she also wrote the words to the hymn *Morning Has Broken*. The Children's Book Circle created the Eleanor Farjeon Award in her memory.

Her remembrances of childhood, love and romance are written down for everyone to read and enjoy. She left a different memory with all of those who knew her: Eleanor Farjeon as a person - full of joy, understanding and compassion, with a unique ability to enhance the lives of everyone she met.

POETRY ANALYSIS

EASTER MONDAY

(In Memoriam E. T.)

This poem is dedicated to Edward Thomas who died on Easter Monday, 9th April 1917. In it, Eleanor Farjeon remembers a letter which she has received from Thomas which had thanked her for a small silver egg which she had sent him as an Easter present. She had obviously sent him a box of apples to remind him of his beloved home, and had concealed the egg amongst them. This simple gift and the thought behind it must have touched Edward Thomas and moved him to write a letter of thanks to Eleanor.

She recalls that on that occasion, Easter Monday had been a seemingly glorious spring day during which she had spent some time in the garden (presumably at the family home in Fellows Road). She remarks on the outward signs of the coming of spring. Edward's letter had been written on the eve of a battle, and this sense of impending doom is reiterated in the second verse as Eleanor realises that after this day, her life will be changed for ever - it was the following evening that she learned of Edward's death. She remembers the letters she has written to him which he will never receive.

This poem was written after its given date of 9th April 1917, but it is *about* that day, and shows the impact of the death of Edward Thomas on Eleanor Farjeon. She saw him not only as the great unrequited love of her life, but also as a soulmate: someone with whom she had so much to share - their love of poetry, the countryside and nature.

The tone of *Easter Monday* is similar to that employed by many other home-front poets, such as Vera Brittain and Edith Nesbit. There is an element of regret for what has been lost and Eleanor Farjeon mingles this sadness with fond memories of the person who has died. Like Edith Nesbit in *The Fields of Flanders*, Eleanor also mentions the joy and hope that come with the arrival of each new spring before reminding us of the sorrow that would come to dominate the lives of those left behind.

PEACE

In this poem, Eleanor Farjeon begins by describing the various
attributes of peace, which, it would seem, she does not view as an
entirely positive or permanent state. She compares peace with war,
describing both in similar terms. Peace, she implies, is merely one of
the inevitable consequences of war. In peacetime memories of war
are like an ugly scar which serves only to remind the survivors of
the madness that has gone before. Her description of the war as
glamourous is interesting as many young men (and women) had
thought of the war in those terms, particularly in the early days. Yet
once the fighting dies down, battles can be viewed more realistically
and war does not seem glamourous any more. It becomes clear
that Eleanor regards peace as a mere interlude between wars. This,
she says, should be a time for reflection and for counting the cost.
Peace should provide an opportunity for men to re-evaluate their
position and take stock - to look back on what has happened with a
more critical eye - as historians will do in years to come.

Eleanor asserts that all nations are to blame - they are greedy for
growth and victory and they do not care how many generations of
men must be sacrificed in the process of achieving their aims. She
believes that peace shines a revealing light on the ambitions of the
warmongers, which should enable them to see the consequences of
their actions. However, she appears to believe that these nations
behave more like predators than the conventional doves of peace:
preferring to pursue a course of hatred than one of love and
friendship.

Next, Eleanor paints an even more negative picture of peace. War,
she says, is a crime - and the only righteous quality of peace is to
put an end to this senseless activity. In peacetime, the fear of death
and war is finished, but again she implies that this relaxation is a
temporary state and that peace can bring even more uncertainty

than war. Although in times of war the people must learn to cope with their anxieties, at least they know what it is that they are afraid of. Peace brings a different type of apprehension - one which, if allowed to develop, can paralyse the nation in fear, just as if it had looked upon the face of Medusa and turned to stone. (Medusa was a character, known as a Gorgon, in Greek mythology who had snakes for hair and eyes that turned the beholder to stone). Eleanor seems to imply that the warmongers believe the only way to avert this stagnation is war and the nationalist fervour which war promotes.

Peace gives men more freedom and allows individual countries to prove themselves as worthy, or otherwise, by their actions and reactions. Finally Eleanor challenges the war-loving nations to put an end to talk of hatred and speak instead of love. However, she puts her final point in the form of a question, which remains unanswered. This suggests that she does not hold out much hope that her request will be heard or adhered to.

This thought-provoking poem is a harsh indictment on those responsible for the war. Eleanor Farjeon does not seem to blame any one particular country or group of countries, but she asserts that all nations involved should share an equal burden of responsibility. Somewhat prophetically, she sees such periods of peace as a mere pause in the fighting which she thinks will inevitably continue until such time as one nation has the courage to put aside their fears and hatred and build a future based on love and hope.

'NOW THAT YOU TOO'

This poem is addressed to a soldier who is about to embark for the front. The soldier in question may have been Edward Thomas, although there is no evidence for this, or the poem may have been directed more generally, to the many men who went away to war, and the women they left behind.

The second and third lines of the first verse are particularly interesting: Eleanor Farjeon describes the war-years in terms of bloodshed and weariness; she implies that the number of dead is so vast that it cannot even be counted and that every day brings news of another hoard who have vanished and will never return. She re-asserts this by suggesting that the world will never know this number of young men again. In this she seems to be implying that the war will have far-reaching and costly consequences for generations to come.

Then, in the desperate tones of a young lover, she reminds us of the sorrow of parting - the effort required not to spoil a final meeting by dwelling too much on what might happen, but struggling to enjoy a last farewell, while holding on to happy memories. She remembers that, while both parties are mortal, their love for each other is not and this will live on in the future, whatever that may bring.

Even if this poem is not addressed to one particular soldier, the description of a final farewell is very poignantly written. The hopeless anguish of saying goodbye to a loved-one for the last time comes through especially well in this poem because at the beginning, we are told that there is no hope - so many have gone this way before. The description of seeing, hearing and feeling everything for the last time, implies that if he dies, her life will also end and yet she is resigned to this because their fate lies elsewhere.

Thus, although this is a sad and reflective poem, which begins
with talk of death, fear and loss, it ends on a more positive note -
of love.

WINIFRED M LETTS

BIOGRAPHY

Born in 1882 in County Wexford, Ireland, Winifred Letts was educated at St Anne's Abbots in Bromley and then at Alexandra College in Dublin. Her parents lived in Blackrock, County Dublin.

During the First World War, Winifred served as a Voluntary Aid Detachment nurse in Manchester. She went on to become a masseuse, joining the Almeric Paget Military Massage Corps. Later, she married William Henry Foster Verschoyle and they lived together in Dublin and then in Faversham in Kent, where Winifred remained until her death in 1972.

William Verschoyle had been married before and had lost two sons in the First World War. Francis Stuart died, aged 19, in April 1915 and William Arthur died almost exactly two years later, at the age of 27.

Winifred was a prolific writer, her first book, *The Story Spinner*, being published in 1907. She wrote stories, children's books, plays and poems.

POETRY ANALYSIS

THE DESERTER

This poem tells the story of a young man, so overcome with fear that he runs away from the fighting and is executed for desertion.

We learn that this man has been afraid for a long time and that this fear has become overwhelming. Winifred Letts compares his fear with that of a frightened child or a hunted animal, who will do anything in his desperation to escape, regardless of the consequences. This man would have known that the penalty for desertion was execution by firing squad, but he chooses to opt for the certainty of death, rather than the uncertainty of continuing at the front, never knowing when or in what form his death will come.

The author urges us not to judge this man and then, somewhat ambiguously, speaks of the shame one feels in witnessing a man thus overcome with fear. To her the "irony of life" is not that this young man died anyway, despite his attempts to escape, or that he died at the hands of his fellow Englishmen, but that his mother believes he died a hero and remains unaware of the reality of her son's death. Winifred Letts seems to be implying that the mother is better off not knowing how her son died.

This poem judges the young soldier quite harshly - his name is unimportant and not worth mentioning, and while the author claims not to judge him, she also appears to show little sympathy for his plight, pointing out that even in death, he has chosen a blindfold (possibly seen as a cowardly option), as she says that the men cannot see his eyes. The reason for this attitude is possibly that many of those at home preferred to believe that men should fight bravely and never show fear. It is, after all, more acceptable to suppose that the soldiers were going, happily, to their deaths, than that they were terrified out of their wits. In the case of Winifred Letts, this feeling would probably have been enhanced by her work as a VAD which would have brought her into close contact with men who had been injured in the trenches. For a man to try to desert his position would have seemed shameful to her, when she was faced every day with men who had accepted their wounds with stoicism. For a woman at home during the war, even one serving as a nurse, the realities of trench life were often impossible to comprehend.

This poem bears some comparison with Siegfried Sassoon's *The Hero*, which also deals with the fate of a soldier attempting to evade the fighting. Sassoon's hero is given a name, Jack, which gives him an identity and makes him seem more human to the reader, and although he has not been executed, his death is not seen by his fellow men as one of heroism, since he had panicked and become hysterical at the explosion of a mine. Again, Jack's mother is deluded into believing that her son died a hero and this helps her to cope with her grief. Sassoon's sympathies are different from those of Winifred Letts, however, since through his use of satire and irony, he seems to be questioning the importance placed on the manner of a soldier's death, rather than the death itself.

SCREENS (In a Hospital)

Written, probably, from first-hand experience, this poem tells the story of the death of a soldier in hospital. The placing of screens around the dying man's bed denote his impending demise, but when this happens, he is replaced by yet another wounded man.

The screens are placed round the young soldier's bed in order to afford him some privacy and dignity and also to protect the other wounded men in the hospital ward from witnessing his death. The hospital ward must be kept quiet, so the nurses play cards, instead of listening to music, while the young man dies. We are informed of the soldier's extreme youth and the fact that his life has hardly begun. The author tells us where the soldier was wounded, which makes this poem easier to date. (The attack at Sulva Bay was part of the ill-fated Gallipoli campaign and took place in August 1915). The continuous flow of wounded men is also mentioned as the poet points out that this bed will soon be taken by another.

Again, this poem seems quite harsh: the man is not named or even described in any detail which gives him a sense of anonymity; the nurses play at cards while the man is left to die alone; the contrast is made between the red colour of the screens and the whiteness of the sheets that cover the dying man, demonstrating that the innocence of his youth has been surpassed by what he has witnessed in the war, including death and destruction.

The description of the soldiers' injuries, being given in the weight of the lead shot, makes his wounds seem quite mechanical or technical, and less human. The mention of the Union Jack, which will cover him when he is dead, is the only hint at patriotism in the poem, although it is unclear whether the poet views his death as glorious or wasteful.

Finally, the soldier dies and is replaced by another wounded man, which is, again a mechanical way of looking at the situation. The poet points out that the nurses (and other patients, for that matter) will be able to make some noise again, meaning that their lives will be able to return to normal. This affords a sense of insignificance to the soldier's death. The regret expressed in the final line, although this could be interpreted as ironic, seems almost light-hearted and the reader certainly does not gain the impression that the author has been adversely influenced by the death of this soldier. This might seem harsh, but could also be interpreted as a nurse's means of remaining detached from the suffering which surrounded her; or equally, as a way of showing, through satire, the monotonous nature of hospital life: as one soldier dies, he is replaced by another who will probably die too.

WHAT REWARD?

This short poem contrasts the "reward" for example, the mourning and, in some cases, over glorification of those who have died, and the care and attention given to those who have been physically maimed, compared with those who have suffered in a more hidden, psychological manner.

Winifred Letts seems to be saying that those who have given their sanity have made the greatest sacrifice of all. The dead are seen as glorious; the maimed can rest and will be looked after and lauded as heroes. However, the young men who emerged from the war with deep psychological scars, for whom life would never be the same again, were treated very differently. These men were less tolerable to a society which found mental illness somewhat embarrassing. Sometimes these men were locked away; they were certainly never paraded as heroic figures who had given as much, if not more, than their physically wounded comrades.

It should also be noted that, at this stage, there was a limited understanding of the mental breakdown which such traumas could cause, and men who suffered thus were often accused of shirking their responsibilities. This poem cries out against the injustice of this situation: these poor men are no less deserving of our thoughts than those more "acceptably" or "conventionally" wounded.

What Reward? could be compared with Siegfried Sassoon's *Glory of Women*, which describes how proud and pleased those at home are when soldiers are wounded (provided that the wound is not in an embarrassing place), or even killed, and how such men are treated with deference and respect. The public, Sassoon points out, react with disbelief at the idea of a man becoming mentally broken by his experiences and shy away from the realisation that such things could even happen.

Both poets are stating that no matter what the wound is, or how it is gained, all the damaged soldiers are worthy of equal remembrance and praise.

CHARLOTTE MEW

BIOGRAPHY

The turbulent life of Charlotte Mew began on 15th November 1869 in Doughty Street, off Gray's Inn Road in London. Her father, Frederick, was an architect from Newport on the Isle of Wight. Her mother, Anna Maria Kendall Mew came from London. Frederick had become an architectural assistant to Anna's father in 1857, and the couple married six years later. Theirs was to be a long marriage, overshadowed by great tragedy. Anna was, reputedly, a rather shallow woman, who firmly believed, throughout her matrimonial life, that she had married beneath her. She did very little around the house, preferring to leave all domestic chores to the servants. When the couple's first child, Henry, was born in 1865, a nurse, named Elizabeth Goodman, was employed.

Two years later, another son, Frederick, was born. That summer the family took a holiday in Broadstairs and it was here that young Frederick contracted an infection and died at the age of two months.

As stated previously, Charlotte was born on 15th November 1869. In 1871 another son, Richard, was born, followed in 1873 by Caroline Frances Anne, who was known throughout her life by her third Christian name. Another son, Daniel (also known as Christopher) was born in 1875.

The following year was a particularly tragic one for the Mews. Young Christopher died in March, aged just four months old. There seems to be some mystery surrounding the cause of his death. It is certified that the infant died from 'convulsions', although it is not clear whether these were the result of an infection or some congenital defect. Then, in early December, Richard, aged five years, died of Scarlet Fever.

The youngest child, Freda, was born in 1879. It would appear that Freda had some sort of mental instability which manifested itself from an early age, although the precise nature of this affliction is not recorded. Henry, the oldest child, was similarly affected and in approximately 1888, he was committed to Peckham House Lunatic Asylum. It is believed that he had, for many years, suffered from some form of dementia, which eventually caused his family to have him committed to this institution. Freda was also placed in a Lunatic Asylum, probably in 1897, at the age of sixteen. Upon her father's insistence, young Freda, who it is believed was suffering from schizophrenia, was committed to the Isle of Wight Asylum. This was in order that she could be close to her father's family, who still resided on the Island.

During all of this tragedy and upheaval, Charlotte was educated at the Gower Street School, run by Lucy Harrison. The family would take annual holidays to the Isle of Wight, although their mother would only accompany them as far as Brighton, preferring to remain there with her friends, while Elizabeth Goodman proceeded with the children. Sometime in 1888 the family moved from Doughty Street to Number 9 Gordon Street, Gordon Square in London WC1. This house was later destroyed in the Blitz bombings of the Second World War.

In 1894 Charlotte's story *Passed* was published in *The Yellow Book - An Illustrated Quarterly*. This story tells of an imaginary walk from Charlotte's familiar London streets into the poorer districts of the Capital, and describes the scenes she witnesses en-route.

Shortly after arranging Freda's committal to the Isle of Wight Asylum, Charlotte's father died from stomach cancer. He had always been an extravagant man and died, leaving no capital for his surviving wife and children to live on. Their mother had a small inheritance in her own right, but Frederick's death ensured that the family's financial circumstances were quite dire.

Anne had become an artist and she took work restoring paintings and antique furniture, although she was paid poorly for her services. Over the next few years, Charlotte published several stories and poems in various magazines and periodicals. The earnings supplied by the two sisters provided much-needed income for the family.

In 1901 Henry, Charlotte's oldest brother, died in Peckham House Lunatic Asylum from tuberculosis. Charlotte's mother became increasingly dependant on her two surviving daughters. If they decided to go away for a while on a holiday, she would employ a companion. However, should the companion prove unsatisfactory, she would immediately summon one of her daughters - usually Charlotte - to return.

Unsurprisingly, the various events in Charlotte's life had a profound effect on her temperament. She had very deep feelings of sorrow about all the unhappiness and torment which had dominated her life. Anne, always the more optimistic of the two, was her constant companion and their 20th Century friends knew very little, if anything, of their earlier tragedies. Sadness seems to have followed Charlotte throughout her personal life. She had an unusual appearance: she was small, almost doll-like, yet she wore men's clothing, kept her hair cut short, smoked and used strong language. When she was allowed, by her demanding mother, the freedom to travel, she did so alone - an unusual course of action for a woman at the turn of the Century. One such journey in 1902 found her in Paris, visiting fellow author Ella D'Arcy. Charlotte was in love with

Ella, but her feelings were not reciprocated and Charlotte, disappointed and rejected, returned to London.

After 1909 Charlotte's writing began to be taken more seriously. She was rapidly becoming a popular and critically acclaimed writer and poet. She continued to publish stories and poems, and was encouraged to give poetry readings. Her professional success was tempered by further unhappiness in her private life. In 1913, at one of her readings, Charlotte met fellow writer, May Sinclair. Although there would seem to have been a close friendship between these two women, May rejected Charlotte's romantic advances and then, it is alleged, publicly humiliated Charlotte for having thus approached her in the first place.

Fortunately Charlotte's new-found literary friends, such as Harold Monro and his assistant Alida Klemantaski (who would later become his wife), ignored this potential scandal and continued to help her publish her work. This included, in 1916, the publication of a collection of verse under the title *The Farmer's Bride*. This anthology brought her to the attention of Sydney Cockerell, a champion of struggling writers. Cockerell introduced Charlotte to other poets and authors including Thomas Hardy and Siegfried Sassoon who greatly admired her work, often citing her as his favourite woman poet. Sassoon first met Charlotte in June 1919, at Anne's studio. Discovering that the two sisters had little income and an elderly mother to support, Sassoon offered Charlotte paid work - writing reviews for the *Herald*, a newspaper of which he was the Literary Editor.

In 1922, Charlotte, Anne and their mother moved of 86 Delancey Street, Camden Town. The following year, Anna, Charlotte's mother, died - probably from bowel cancer - at the age of 86. Charlotte and Anne, now in their 50's, continued to live together. Neither of them had married and they had both agreed very early in life that neither would have any children, for fear of passing on their family's mental instabilities. Charlotte also had always felt isolated by her sexuality. Unlike homosexuality, lesbianism was not illegal, but it was frowned upon and regarded as socially unacceptable. Charlotte wrote very movingly of her fear, disillusionment and loneliness.

The sisters continued to live quietly, their financial hardship eased slightly by the award, in 1923, of a Civil List Pension to Charlotte. This award, of £75.00 per annum, was achieved by Thomas Hardy, John Masefield and Walter de la Mare lobbying the necessary authorities to recognise the quality of her writing - which they felt had for too long gone unnoticed.

Finally, in June 1927, there came a tragedy from which Charlotte would never recover: Anne died from cancer of the uterus and liver. Charlotte was completely overwhelmed by her grief. She rarely slept and her nerves were seriously affected. She became convinced that Anne had actually been buried alive; she saw 'black spots' in Anne's studio and was certain that these had somehow contributed to her sister's illness - these 'spots' turned out to be specks of soot. Upon her doctor's advice, on 15th February 1928, Charlotte was admitted to a nursing home to be treated for a nervous disorder. Just over one month later, on 24th March, Charlotte took her own life by drinking half a bottle of disinfectant. At the inquest into her death, her doctor said that following Anne's death, Charlotte had become obsessed that she was surrounded by the germs which she believed had killed her sister.

Charlotte Mew was described in one obituary as a 'poet of rare quality', although she never fully appreciated this herself - always having had a low opinion of herself and her own abilities. Others did not share her viewpoint and many in the literary world mourned her death, and hoped that she had finally found the peace she so obviously craved.

POETRY ANALYSIS

THE CENOTAPH
September 1919

Charlotte Mew begins this poem by remembering the wasted land, which will not have had time to re-grow in the ten months since the end of the War. She perceives those fields as one great, deep grave, visited for evermore by those with justifiably proud remembrances of lost loved-ones. At home, however, those who have suffered the deep, slow pain of losing someone close, also need an outward memorial to the dead - this comes in the form of the Cenotaph.

At the foot of this memorial, these mourning people leave flowers, many brought from gardens at home, to demonstrate their grief and remembrance. Charlotte points out that this is the place where those who have no grave can be mourned - they lie with thousands of others in the battlefields, but they can be remembered with flowers and tears here at the Cenotaph.

Memorials, such as this, will appear in market-places all around the country. Throughout the year, while market traders go about their business, the memorials will overshadow them, through the eyes of God and the nation's dead youth.

In July 1919, the original temporary Cenotaph was unveiled as part of the national Peace Day event. There was such an huge public outpouring of grief that the steps of this wood and plaster construction were spontaneously covered with flowers, left by those in mourning. The decision was taken that a permanent memorial should be constructed and work began almost immediately. Charlotte Mew's poem, written in September 1919, reflects this sense of overwhelming loss and the need for a central place or monument upon which the mourning public could focus their grief.

Charlotte Mew demonstrates in this poem some commonly-held sentiments among her generation: gratitude for the sacrifices made by so many, and sadness at the huge waste of life. She appreciates the losses which are being felt by so many whilst demonstrating her own sense of pride in the victory those losses have achieved.

This poem provides an excellent commentary on the events of that time - memorials were being considered and constructed around the country to commemorate the dead and missing of the War; when the Cenotaph was unveiled, people travelled from all over the country to show their respects, often bringing flowers from home to lay in remembrance.

At the end of this poem, however, the tone changes. Charlotte accepts that, for many, life goes on as before. People will continue to go about their daily business, but she seems to have a low opinion of these men and women, referring to them as 'whores' and 'hucksters', which implies an element of compromised principles and a lack of morality on their part. Such people are, she maintains, looked down upon by both God and the dead, whom she regards as having been murdered. She does not state who it is that she considers to be responsible for the fate of these young men, but makes it clear that the loss of so many cannot be ignored or regarded as accidental.

In the same way as the construction of the cenotaph changed the face of Whitehall and formed a permanent reminder of what had happened, Charlotte Mew seems here to be implying that everything has changed - the face of the world has been altered by the cataclysmic events of the War.

MAY, 1915

Although the dated title of this, and the following poem (*June, 1915*), imply that they were written at that time, it is likely that neither was published until 1929, after Charlotte Mew's death. Therefore, to date these poems with any great degree of accuracy is almost impossible.

This short poem essentially speaks of the hope that the war will soon be over and peace will, once again, dominate over pain and death. Even to those who are currently overwhelmed by grief, there must be some hope of a brighter future, although that time has not yet come.

The months of April and May 1915 saw heavy fighting at the Second Battle of Ypres, made famous by the first use, by the Germans, of Chlorine Gas. This battle, which lasted a little over a month, saw many British losses - the dead amounted to nearly 60,000. Charlotte Mew's poem is a reflection of the sadness many felt at that time, yet is tinged optimistically with hope for a brighter future.

Although this poem could be interpreted, quite literally, as a hope for a new Spring, new growth and the re-birth of the earth, it is also open to a slightly different interpretation. The woods, which are described as 'blackened', could be a reference to the dead soldiers, and rather than literally meaning the fallen or broken trees, there could be an implied meaning here of the wounded men, who wait patiently, because that is all they can do, for their health to return, and, ultimately, for peace to come again. In this new, fearful and uncertain world of theirs, the only things of which they can be sure are their natural surroundings.

Then, her thoughts turn to those at home, who sit, blindly oblivious to everything which is going on around them, because they are consumed by grief for their lost loved-ones. Even for these, she asserts, there must be some hope that the world will survive and begin again.

This is a poem of hope, tinged with uncertainty - although she hopes for spring, she seems to be questioning whether or not it will come. Written about - and possibly during - a time when there was little hope for an early conclusion to the hostilities, this poem may seem to contain a slightly unrealistic aspiration. However, the hope for peace was all that many women had to keep them going in the face of such heavy losses.

To equate the coming of peace with the arrival of Spring is a metaphor used by many poets, such as Edith Nesbit in *The Fields of Flanders* - which was written in 1915, and Sara Teasdale in *'There Will Come Soft Rains'*.

At the end of this poem, although Charlotte Mew still talks, hopefully, of more promising times, she acknowledges that for those suffering and mourning the death of a loved-one, such hopes are impossible to realise. These people are not even aware of their surroundings or what is happening around them, let alone being able to look, with any degree of hope, towards the future.

JUNE, 1915

This poem asks a relatively simple, yet unanswered, question - essentially, how can everyday life carry on as before, given the destruction of the world which carries on all around, despite the passage of time.

This is a simple, yet effective, poem which asks how anyone can be expected to think of everyday events during these times. Only for innocent young children is there any continuation of normality. The passage of time, the blossoming of a new flower, are insignificant events when compared to the dreadfulness of the war.

For everyone else, the only things that matter are either surviving one's grief, or dreading the arrival of bad news. She compares the young child reaching out his hand to touch an early rose-bud to the distance of the stars. Both are seen as fearless, yet, to the adults, both the child and the stars are distant - almost incomprehensibly unaware of what is happening around them.

It seems as though witnessing the fear and suffering of those at home has become too much for Charlotte, whose early life was greatly affected by death and illness - perhaps watching others grieving for a lifetime had become more than she could bear, making her long for the innocence of childhood - an innocence which she probably never experienced fully herself.

Finally, she wonders how important the war is, or should be, to the young child whose innocence is so short-lived. She appears to be asking why he shouldn't be allowed to enjoy his childhood? Why should death and destruction dominate absolutely everything?

This poem bears some comparison with *Lament* by Wilfrid Wilson Gibson. Gibson's beautifully moving poem asks similar questions:

namely, how can those who survive the war ever be expected to carry on a normal life again? The main difference between the two poems is that Gibson appears to be saying that if the survivors of the conflict truly understand and appreciate the sacrifices being made on their behalf, their lives can never be the same again. Charlotte Mew, on the other hand, suggests that, while the lives of the adults are, naturally, dominated and affected by the war, why should the children suffer a similar fate? There is enough fear and unhappiness without allowing the sweet and short-lived innocence of youth to be lost forever.

EDITH NESBIT

BIOGRAPHY

Edith Nesbit was born on 19th August 1858. Her father, John Collis Nesbit, a teacher and director of the family's agricultural school in London, died when Edith was four years old. Edith, her mother, Sarah and her brothers and sisters moved away from London, going, initially, to the South Coast. Edith attended boarding school, which she disliked intensely. After a few years, Edith, her mother and her sisters, moved to France, while her brothers were placed in boarding schools in England. Despite a nomadic existence, most of Edith's education was completed in France.

The family returned to England in 1872, settling in Kent. Three years later, when Edith was 17, she and her mother moved back to London - her sister, Mary had died of tuberculosis in 1871, and her brothers, Henry and Alfred, had by now left home.

In 1877, Edith met Hubert Bland, a bank clerk, and the couple embarked on an unconventional relationship which resulted in their marriage three years later, when Edith was seven months pregnant with Hubert's child. Bland, however, also continued to have a relationship with another woman. Edith and Hubert had three children over the next five years and Edith, through her writing and other enterprises also became the main breadwinner in the household.

Edith and her husband were both actively involved in the Fabian Society, of which they were founder members, and jointly edited the society's journal entitled *Today*.

Theirs was a very unconventional and 'open' marriage, during which they both had relationships with other people. Hubert had an affair with the assistant secretary of the Fabian Society, Alice Hoatson. Later, when Alice gave birth to Hubert's daughter, Rosamund, Edith took the unusual step of accepting the situation and bringing this child up as her own.

Edith Nesbit wrote poetry and novels for adults, short stories and plays, but is best remembered for her children's stories, such as: *The Treasure Seekers, The Wouldbegoods, Five Children and It, The Pheonix and the Carpet* and, of course, *The Railway Children*.

Hubert died in 1914, and Edith married Thomas Tucker, a ship's engineer. This decision was not met with favourably by her family and friends who deemed that Tucker, although kindly, was a poor match for Edith, who continued to write until her death on 4th May 1924 from cancer. Edith Nesbit is buried at St Mary in the Marsh at Romney Marsh in Kent.

POETRY ANALYSIS

SPRING IN WAR-TIME

This nature poem describes the sense of loss felt at the passing of a loved-one, presumably a boyfriend or fiancé, and of the experiences which the survivor will no longer be able to enjoy.

This is a poem which tells of lost love and regret. The descriptions of spring-time experiences evoke images of new life, which at the end of each verse are extinguished with the realisation that these activities will either never happen again, or will never be the same. This couple will no longer walk down lover's lane; the violets have lost their scent; they will never build a home or family together.

Each verse describes a different event in the spring - the blossoming and regrowth which occur in that season are contrasted with the knowledge that life, for this woman, has effectively ceased. The everyday occurrences and observations of one left at home, are made extraordinary because she now views them, not with happiness or hope, but with regret for what might have been.

There is a great, but almost unspoken, contrast in this poem between birth and death; beginnings and endings. Spring sees the earth being reborn and coming back to life after the cold winter. War, on the other hand, demonstrates the finality of death - it is as if the earth itself is dying, or is certainly, in mourning.

The final verse shows that this soldier has only recently perished: no flowers have yet grown on his grave, so the writer perceives no sense of hope, or fulfilment of the past and is, as yet, unable to look forward.

This poem is reminiscent of *Perhaps* by Vera Brittain which, similarly, recounts events which the writer feels she will either never know, or will never enjoy again, because her fiancé has died.

This acute sense of loss and loneliness, represented by both these poems, shows the deep and mournful pain and hopelessness which many have experienced as a result of war.

THE FIELDS OF FLANDERS

This poem, through comparisons between war and death, with the beauty of nature, describes the effect of the conflict on the natural surroundings.

In the first verse, the writer describes a lovely scene from the previous spring. The use of rhyme and repetition help promote a sense of pleasure and happiness, which is then shattered in the second verse. Here Edith Nesbit reminds us that all of nature's beauty is gone; the flowers and hedges have been destroyed and replaced by black crosses marking the graves of the dead.

In the third stanza, we are reminded that it is not merely nature's world which is being changed, but also the lives of those who remain. Nothing will remain untouched.

Then, in the fourth verse, the writer remembers that nature will, eventually, triumph. The flowers will return and life will appear to be renewed. The crosses and memories of the dead will, however, always be present to remind us of what has been lost.

Finally, she admits that she does not judge the enemy, but leaves this to God. These words are written with a hint almost of anger at the damage being wrought upon her beloved country. The final two lines of this poem are a desperate admission that the sacrifice being asked, and offered, by so many, is too great.

This is a beautiful, stirring poem, which conjures up images of serenity, together with a sense of gratitude towards those who have served.

It could be argued that Edith Nesbit was writing of the destruction of a physical country and, indeed, that the country she describes may, in fact, be France. She spent many years in France as a child, and may well have been greatly saddened by the devastation being caused there by the war. She is unlikely to have been writing about England as a country, being as her description of the land being destroyed would not tally with the fact that England was not a field of war.

One could argue, however, that she is not speaking of a physical country at all, but of the nation's people. Her descriptions could all relate to people, as well as nature: the beauty described could be that of loved-ones; the memories of last spring may be those of days spent in youth, with one now departed. The tree of life, hedges, flowers and fields, which have been trampled, could refer to the generation of men who have been lost: a way of life which has disappeared. The affects of this war, she avers, are as far-reaching as the destruction of nature itself. New life will, eventually, and naturally reappear, she agrees, but at what cost? A cost which, she obviously feels, can never be repaid.

JESSIE POPE

BIOGRAPHY

Jessie Pope was born in the spring of 1868 in Leicester. Her father, Richard, was a commercial traveller. Jessie and her parents, together with her four siblings, Mary, Charles, Elizabeth and Frank lived initially in Leicester. At that time, Jessie, who was the fourth of the five children, was educated at Craven House School. Later, her father became a Hop Merchant and the family moved to Hornsey in Middlesex and Jessie attended the North London Collegiate School.

By the turn of the century, the family were living in Hampstead and Jessie had become a writer of fiction, light verse and children's books, contributing many poems and to the satirical magazine *Punch*. In addition to this she also regularly contributed articles to newspapers including the *Daily Mail* and the *Daily Express*.

Jessie Pope went on to edit *The Ragged Trousered Philanthropists*, a novel by Robert Tressell. She also published three volumes of war poetry: *War Poems* (1915), *More War Poems* (1915), and *Simple Rhymes for Stirring Times* (1916).

She was married to Mr Edward Babington Lenton and lived to the age of 73, dying in the autumn of 1941 in Okehampton in Devon.

POETRY ANALYSIS

INTRODUCTION - JESSIE POPE'S REPUTATION AS A WAR POET

Jessie Pope's main claim to fame as regards First World War Literature, is that Wilfred Owen originally dedicated his poem *Dulce et Decorum Est* to her. He amended this dedication to read "To a certain poetess", when it was suggested to him that it might be unwise to address her specifically by name.

Jessie Pope's work is often studied now, not because she was a particularly fine poet, but because of Owen's dedication and, therefore, his perceived dislike of her; and also because her work is seen as being representative of many of those left at home who wrote patriotic verse in support of the war. She is often criticised for the tone of her poems: such criticism is not necessarily fair.

Her published works were mainly produced before or during 1916, when many male poets were still producing fervent poems justifying the conflict, paying little heed to the human cost. Julian Grenfell believed that those who died fighting would be made greater by the experience, while Rupert Brooke spoke of the glory of England and the sacrifices required to maintain his country's greatness. John McCrae whose poem *In Flanders Fields* is possibly the most quoted poem of its time, suggests that the dead will only be able to rest, if the living continue the fight on their behalf. So, if the soldier-poets of the day were themselves writing in this manner, it would seem harsh to judge Jessie Pope for repeating similar sentiments.

A more justified criticism of Pope is that she was goading others into joining the fight, when no such sacrifices were expected of her. In this, however, she was not alone. Many non-combatants, of both sexes, wrote in this manner throughout the war, although many changed their tone after 1916 when the extreme cost of the war had become more apparent to those at home.

If we accept that the poets, of both sexes, were writing from their experiences *at that time*, then Jessie Pope should be no more scorned than her male counterparts. It is interesting to note that in 1914, Wilfred Owen, who had not yet enlisted, was writing about how much sweeter it would be to die in war for one's brothers than to live peacefully in oblivion.

The language of Owen's early poetry demonstrates *his* lack of understanding of the slaughter that was to follow, and makes his later protest against Jessie Pope seem less justified.

Jessie Pope was not the greatest poet of her time, or even the greatest female poet of her time, but she did represent, through her work, the opinions of many on the home front and, as such, her opinions, although often difficult to agree with, should not be derided.

WHO'S FOR THE GAME?

The poem, *Who's For The Game?*, when read today, seems almost appallingly bloodthirsty and war-mongering. In it, Pope describes the war as though it were colourful and enjoyable fight; where the colour is obviously a reference to bloodshed. She repeatedly goads those who haven't joined up to do so, pointing out that the country needs young men to enlist. You could compare this call to arms with the famous poster which featured Lord Kitchener and the statement "Your Country Needs You". Jessie Pope isn't really saying anything different at the end of this poem to Lord Kitchener himself. If anything, his entreaties are more cruel than hers: he had, after all, served during other conflicts and fully understood the meaning of war and the sacrifices it would entail. Jessie Pope could, at least, plead ignorance.

One could, alternatively, argue that Pope's very ignorance is what makes her jingoism distasteful. She urges men into a conflict of which she has little knowledge and less understanding. She was, however, not alone in her lack of awareness. Her poems were popular at the time and were considered fairly representative of the general feeling at home. Many people felt a sense of national pride, even if they had lost a loved-one as evidenced in Sassoon's *The Hero*.

Owen's dedication of *Dulce et Decorum Est* to Jessie Pope or "a certain poetess" was an obvious criticism of the messages contained in poems such as this one. For this reason, many people choose to compare *Who's for the Game?* with *Dulce et Decorum Est*. This is quite understandable as the tone of Pope's work is what provoked Owen's response and his plea that she, and people like her, should stop lying about how sweet and meet it is to die for one's country. The language used in *Dulce et Decorum Est* is deliberately shocking to force those at home - the complacent ones, at least - to realise the truth.

If one must compare these two poets, it is actually just as interesting to compare *Who's for the Game?* with Owen's *Disabled* as they have more in common, which makes the contrasts between them more noteworthy.

Pope's poem is a patriotic appeal to join in the "fun". She continually refers to the war as though it were a football match, referring, for example to sitting in the stands and tackling the job in hand. In particular, one should notice the whistle being blown as a signal to go. This comparison refers to the whistle blown by the referee to start the football match, and also to the whistle which an officer would blow as a signal for the men to leave the trenches and go 'over the top'. Pope asserts that men should feel proud to serve the cause, even if they should be injured. She makes no mention of the possibility of death.

Disabled tells the story of a very young man, who used to enjoy a game of football, even if it meant receiving an injury, and how he liked being carried by his team-mates, at the end of a match, like a hero. This is something which he can no longer do, since he has lost both legs and one arm in the fighting. Owen's poem is all about the consequences of going to war and the fact that death is not the only way to give away your life.

The soldier in *Disabled* sits in his wheelchair trying to remember why he enlisted. He realises that he did it because someone had said he would look good in a kilt and to please Meg, his girlfriend. This brings us back to *Who's for the Game?* where Pope does exactly this; goads the young men into fighting. The problem with this, according to Owen, is that, having served his country and returned home maimed, no-one wants to know this soldier anymore, preferring the men with complete bodies instead; no-one cheers the wounded soldiers, as they cheered them on when they were leaving for the front.

Pope implies that it is more worthy to fight and be maimed, than not to fight at all. Her description of those who refuse to fight as having missed out on the fun, takes us back to the whole war being perceived as a game. Pope would have the reader believe that there are no dreadful consequences to be faced. Contrast this with the soldier in Owen's poem who feels that he has squandered his life by throwing away his legs. All he can do now is sit and remember the fun he used to share with his friends - he can no longer join in any sort of game. He is beginning to doubt whether the loss he has suffered was worth "the cause" for which he went to fight.

Consider also the language of these two poems: *Disabled* is a sad poem, where Owen makes use of colours to depict the difference between past and present. For instance, the present is a grey, cold, colourless environment full of bitterness and regret. The soldier, despite his youth, is in the winter of his life. The past, on the other hand, is portrayed as colourful and bright and such references make that time seem more like summer. *Who's for the Game?* is written in a more jaunty style with no darkness whatsoever. The only reference to colour is in line two of the first verse and, while this could allude to the bloodshed, it is portrayed positively, as something to look forward to. In Pope's poem the only disappointment or sadness would be to have missed out on all the "fun".

SOCKS

Jessie Pope did not write exclusively in an ardently patriotic fashion. Her poem *Socks*, has a completely different tone. There are definite elements of sorrow and regret in this poem which tells of a wife or mother sitting by the fire knitting socks and thinking of her loved-one. She remembers his departure and how he had been close to tears, but this is not said as a criticism, more as an appreciation that he had tried to put a brave face on his sorrow. She worries about him - simple things like whether he's warm enough, and whether he is finding a soldier's life too arduous.

The sudden noise of the paper-boy makes her start - it reminds her of the dreaded knock of the telegram-boy. The woman wonders where her soldier is now, and what he's been doing. The poem ends with the woman optimistically hoping that he'll come home and tell her all about his adventures.

Throughout the poem, Pope ends each stanza with a reference to knitting instructions and the inclusion of these can be interpreted in several ways. Women frequently knitted socks and other items of clothing for the men at the front - not just their own families, but often these garments were sent out en-masse from women's groups. Many women, who for whatever reason were unable to contribute directly to the war-effort, saw this as their way of helping the men at the front, so Pope could simply be reminding us that women were not idly sitting at home, but were doing whatever they could to help the soldiers. Alternatively, she could be pointing out the monotony of life for the women at home - the repetitive knitting pattern symbolises this, and maybe she is making a comparison here between his adventures and potential sacrifices, and her (comparatively) meagre contribution to his well-being. As a third alternative, the knitting could also be seen as an occupation

which keeps the woman from thinking about her worries and fears
- something which keeps her going, and banishes unwelcome
thoughts which might otherwise prove too distracting.

Socks is a far more realistic poem than *War Girls*, for example.
Although both paint a picture of female life during the war, *Socks* at
least allows that women should be allowed to worry about their
men, while getting on with life.

WAR GIRLS

War Girls has a very different tone from many of Jessie Pope's other works. Although still proud and patriotic, the subject matter is not the same. Here, she is not addressing herself to would-be soldiers, goading them to fight for their country, instead this poem is a celebration of the role of women in the war. Pope describes various jobs which, in the absence of men, women have undertaken - for example, the ticket collector, lift operator or driver. She speaks of the pre-war woman as though she were trapped, and has only now gained her freedom. This was, indeed, quite true. Many women, called upon to work for the first time, discovered that staying dutifully at home had, in fact, been a very unfulfilling way of life. At the same time, however, she reminds us that these women must still fulfil their household or womanly duties with a warm heart, and also that many of them are resourceful mothers. The women, she says, are also loyal, having no time for affairs of the heart and thinking only of the return of their fighting men.

This poem is a rose-tinted, optimistic portrayal of what was often a harsh reality: for example, women were not always treated very well by their employers and they, quite often, had to do dangerous work. In addition, Pope makes no mention of the widowed wife or grieving mother. She speaks of the return of the soldiers as a certainty, but her men will be marching, not in wheelchairs or on stretchers. In common with many of her other poems, death is not seen as a necessary consequence of war - in fact it is not even mentioned.

Jessie Pope is often accused of fuelling the jingo-women; the minority of women who gave out white feathers to men who had not joined up. Quite often, these men had been *unable* to enlist, either because their work at home was considered important to the war-effort, or because their health was deemed too poor for them to serve. *War Girls* makes no mention of these women, celebrating instead, those who chose to work, in place of the men, at various tasks not normally allocated to women. However, she also makes no mention of the women who did other war work, such as VAD's, ambulance drivers etc.. As such, it appears that this poem is an attempt to praise only the women who took over the men's work. However, in reality, many of these women were, in fact, not so ready to give up their work and return to their previously subservient way of life when the men returned from the war.

Although this poem is less controversial than *Who's For the Game* or *The Call*, its lack of realism makes it less appealing than perhaps it might have been.

THE CALL

This poem shares a similar theme with much of Pope's other work, particularly *Who's for the Game?* Here, she levels accusations of cowardice against those who choose not to enlist.

Pope uses strong, stirring language in her attempt to whip her readers into a frenzy of nationalistic pride and encourage them to 'do their bit'. She asks a series of questions, urging young men to join up, rather than protect themselves by staying at home. The constant questioning involved in this poem is reminiscent of a nagging wife and has the effect of wearing down the reader to the point of submission.

She gives enlistment and fighting an air of jollity, mentioning banners, drums, processions and victory, while suggesting that even to take part in a battle must be a thrilling honour for those involved. Against this, at the end of each verse, she creates an image of those who are left behind as cowardly, biting their nails, saving their own skin.

Once again, Jessie Pope demonstrates here a lack of understanding, goading others into fighting, and dying for not just their country, but their Empire. Victory seems assured in this poem - no mention is made of defeat, injury or death.

The Call is extremely similar in tone, style and content to *Fall In* by Harold Begbie which was first published in The Daily Chronicle in late August 1914. This is a propaganda poem which was soon set to music. In fact, a whole merchandising campaign was created around popular verses and songs such as this - badges and posters were produced and sold. Begbie's poem is, in many ways, even more disturbing than Pope's. She speaks of loyalty, heroism, patriotism and even 'fun' as being the positive aspects of the war, with the only negative being cowardice. Begbie, on the other hand, urges men to join in the fight simply for fear of what others will think of them if they do not - hardly a sound reason for sacrificing one's life.

Although there is no date given for the composition of *The Call*, the fact that Pope mentions Sir John French in the first verse means that it was definitely written prior to December 1915, when French was replaced by Sir Douglas Haig as Commander in Chief of the British Expeditionary Force. This was prior to the introduction of conscription, and many poets were either officially employed, or saw it as their duty to rally men to join the fight.

IRIS TREE

BIOGRAPHY

Iris Tree came from one of the most influential theatrical families of her time. Her father was the actor-manager, Herbert Beerbohm-Tree and her mother was the actress Helen Maud Holt (who was familiarly known by her second name). Iris's half-uncle was Max Beerbohm, a drama critic, essayist and caricaturist.

Herbert and Maud married in 1882, when he was a 26 year old aspiring actor and Maud was an insecure 19 year old orphan. Herbert adopted the name 'Tree' as a stage name, after his father, disappointed at his son's choice of profession, had told him that he should always aspire to reach the top of the tree.

In July 1884 their first child, Viola, was born. In the ten years between this and the birth of her sister, Felicity, Maud and Herbert embarked on theatrical tours of America as well as performances in London and the provinces. Gradually, Herbert began to become more influential and wealthy, until in 1887 he was in a position to fulfil his ambition of becoming an actor-manager by taking a lease on the Haymarket Theatre in London. His role also expanded to take in more directing and this was something which invariably caused friction between Herbert and Maud. She felt that he was unnecessarily harsh in his criticism of her performances while paying too much attention to the other actresses. Her suspicions of his extra-marital activities were fuelled by anonymous letters which she received informing her of his affairs. When Maud brought these to Herbert's attention, rather than denying the affairs, or changing his ways, he suggested that in future, she should send all correspondence to their lawyer.

Opposite the Haymarket Theatre was the site of a former opera house and in 1896 Herbert purchased this. With the help of investors, he built Her Majesty's Theatre, which he named in honour of the Queen. To this day, in fact, the theatre changes its name according to whether there is a king or queen on the throne. Her Majesty's, which opened in April 1897, was an elegant building, both inside and out, with a copper dome which housed a small apartment where Herbert and Maud hosted supper parties after opening nights. They also used the apartment to entertain literary and theatrical guests, such as Oscar Wilde.

Late in 1896, while the building work on the new theatre was still ongoing, Herbert departed on another tour of America. Maud, who was by now settled at 77 Sloane Street, was unable to accompany him because she was expecting their third child. The couple both longed for a son, but another daughter, Iris, was born on 27th January 1897. Herbert was still in America, but Maud wrote to a friend that any disappointment she felt at having a third daughter was short-lived, especially as the new baby had such a sunny and happy nature.

Iris' childhood had an air of the fairytale about it. She and her sisters were frequently allowed backstage at the theatre, together with family friends, such as Diana Manners. This upbringing made Iris long for romance and adventure. She was keenly aware that she was the plainest of the three sisters, but resolved that although she was the 'ugly ducking', she would do whatever was required to become a 'swan', and always took a great deal of interest in her appearance.

In 1904 Herbert founded the Royal Academy of Dramatic Art (RADA) at His Majesty's Theatre (the name had changed as Edward VII was now King), and it was here that Viola completed her education before joining her father on the stage. Felicity and Iris were to have been educated at home, but this idea was abandoned when 25 successive governesses failed to match up to Maud's exacting standards. The two girls were, therefore, enrolled at Miss Wolff's day school in South Audley Street. It was here that Iris first met Nancy Cunard, and also began to develop her interest in English Literature. She gained top marks in the school, although she was one of the youngest girls there. The pupils at Miss Wolff's were not segregated by age or ability but were all taught together in the drawing room of the large house.

Every year a Christmas party was held at the theatre where there would be a special performance for the girls, their friends and their parents. After the show, everyone was allowed backstage to meet the actors, such as Ellen Terry and there followed a sumptuous feast in the dome. Also each Christmas, the Trees would visit other families, although Iris always felt out-of-place and gauche in these grand houses.

In 1909, Herbert received a knighthood and the family moved into Walpole House in Chiswick Mall. This was a romantic and elegant house, made even more so by Maud's tasteful decoration. Viola became a welcome member of the 'Corrupt Coterie' - a group of young intellectuals, founded by the Manners sisters, together with Julian and Gerald ('Billy') Grenfell and the Asquith children, among others. Iris had by now begun writing poetry, some of which was brought to the attention of Herbert Asquith - the Prime Minister - who expressed his appreciation of her poetic talents.

Viola gave up the stage in 1912 and went to Italy to train as an opera singer. Before she left, she also became secretly engaged to Alan Parsons, a handsome, intelligent Oxford graduate who, being the son of the Rector of Tandridge in Surrey, was deemed by Maud to be an unsuitable match for her eldest daughter. During her stay in Italy, Viola rented a little house with fellow student, Maria Schwelter. These two were soon joined by Iris, who had been sent there by her parents in order to study music and drawing. Although her teachers soon discovered that Iris had the better voice, she lacked Viola's dedication and showed no inclination towards formal studies.

Viola and Maria were engaged to perform at a provincial opera house, and were obliged to leave 15 year old Iris at the rented house, in the care of a housekeeper. This gave Iris almost too much freedom and her letters at that time demonstrate that she had developed a very free-spirit, fancying herself in love with a young handsome Italian with whom she spent a great deal of time alone, and receiving love-letters from other young men. Any great scandal was avoided, however, when Herbert summoned Viola back to England to play the lead in *Orpheus In the Underworld*. The two sisters, Maria and the housekeeper duly returned to London. Here Viola discovered that her mother no longer objected to Alan Parsons as a potential son-in-law, so the couple were married in July 1912 at St Martin's in the Fields.

With her childhood now essentially behind her, Iris began to fully appreciate what a happy time it had been, like a wondrous fairytale, secure and happy with affectionate parents whom she loved dearly.

While growing up, however, all three girls had come to realise that their father's philandering caused great unhappiness to their mother. Maud gained some temporary relief from this when a popular and talented member of the theatre company, Lewis Waller, fell in love with her. They refrained from embarking on an affair since he was also married, but through his attentions, Maud regained her self-confidence and her sense of humour - even managing to joke with friends about her husband's infidelity. Her happiness was short-lived, however, as she was soon involved in a car accident which broke her jaw. This not only ended her career as a leading lady, but the permanent disfigurement had a profound psychological effect as she had always placed great importance on physical appearances. The only positive aspect of this event was that Herbert became more attentive and compassionate. Although still unwilling to give up his philandering, he became much more discreet, trying to protect Maud from further unnecessary pain.

Iris's wild behaviour had continued since her return from Italy and, in an attempt to calm her down, her parents sent her to the countryside to stay with her married cousin to whom they issued strict instructions regarding their daughter's behaviour. The idea that she needed taming infuriated Iris, who in a defiant act of rebellion, cut off her golden plait of hair and left it on a train, thus becoming one of the first girls in England to appear with bobbed hair.

The summers of 1913 and 1914 were spent in a rented house on the banks of the Seine. When the First World War was declared, the family hurried back to England. During their journey, Maud became separated from the main party and when she arrived at Victoria Station many hours later, she was relieved and gratified to find Herbert waiting for her, full of genuine concern and apprehension.

Iris was, by now, attending the Slade School of Art, and continued to do so despite the war. She enjoyed being the centre of attention and her mode of dress, independent streak and unpredictable behaviour certainly made her a noticeable student. At this time she and Nancy Cunard rented a studio flat where they secretly met friends, drank, smoked and discussed art and poetry, away from any disapproving parental glare. One morning, after a particularly indulgent night, Iris and Nancy jumped, fully clothed, into the Serpentine, and were promptly arrested by a passing policeman. When their parents were informed, the young ladies were forced to confess to the existence of the studio and their keys were confiscated. Undeterred, both girls had new keys cut and continued with their high life.

Iris attended many parties, but usually felt uncomfortable amongst 'society' types. One notable exception to this was at the parties given by Lady Ottoline Morell. Here she was at home, being amongst people who dressed as eccentrically as she did, and who held similar views to her. She met, and became friends with Augustus John and Sybil Hart-Davis who was 10 years older than Iris, married and much more conventional, but who went on to become Iris' greatest confidante. Through Augustus John, she also met Horace de Vere Cole, a renowned practical joker. He and Iris enjoyed many late night adventures which usually bordered on the criminal.

Another young man who caught Iris' eye was her cousin Evelyn Beerbohm. Felicity, although normally more interested in sportsmen and soldiers, shared her sister's interest in Evelyn and a rivalry developed between the two of them. As the war progressed, however, their lives were touched by death as one by one, many of their friends were killed, including Julian and Gerald ('Billy') Grenfell, and later Raymond Asquith and Edward Wyndham Tennant. One friend who survived was Sir Matthew 'Scatters' Wilson, who left for Gallipoli with a locket containing a photograph of Iris around his neck.

Late in 1915, Iris accompanied Herbert to California where he was commissioned to play Macbeth in a film. Just before leaving, Maud informed Iris that her father had two illegitimate sons living in America. Iris was undisturbed by this news, even when one of Herbert's sons met them from the boat. Her embarrassed father, however, insisted that they should refer to one another as cousins.

Herbert and Iris grew closer during this trip. He worked hard on his filming, but found time to deliver speeches urging the United

States to support the Allied war effort and he was most shocked to discover that Iris was a pacifist. While in America, they dined with Charlie Chaplin, who idolised Herbert and became a close friend to both him and Iris. When the filming was completed, Herbert appeared on the New York stage in *Oliver Twist*, playing Fagin to Chaplin's Artful Dodger. Then Herbert embarked on a grand Shakespearean tour, beginning in Boston. It was here that he met and became romantically involved with Solita Solano, a 25 year old journalist and drama critic. When Herbert left Boston to begin his tour, Iris returned to New York, During his absence she met a painter named Curtis Moffat. She spent all of her time with him and was soon passionately in love.

Almost immediately upon Herbert's return to New York, Iris announced her intention of marrying Moffat. Herbert refused to allow this, saying that Curtis was too poor and they were both too young to entertain such an idea. In December 1916, he resumed his tour and Iris returned to her lover. Together, they attended a party where the Mayor was present and asked him to perform the marriage ceremony on the spot. When he heard of this, Herbert was mortified by his daughter's actions and persuaded the couple to hold a more traditional ceremony, which they agreed to, enabling him to send news of her 'engagement' to the London press. All three of his daughters had, therefore, married despite initial parental disapproval - Felicity had married Geoffrey Cory-Wright while he was on leave, having been wounded at the front, although she had actually become secretly engaged to him before the war, while he was still at Cambridge.

Iris and Curtis took their honeymoon in Nassau, where they remained for some time. Iris was deliriously happy and she was unwilling to break this spell of contentment, especially as she had also discovered that she was pregnant. The couple decided that due to Iris's condition they should be nearer to a town and it's amenities, so they travelled to Havana. Upon their arrival, however, Curtis became ill and was admitted to a nursing home, where Iris remained with him.

That summer, his tour complete and his daughter happily married, Herbert decided to return to England. He did so via Spain, where he was informed that Lloyd George, who was by now the Prime Minister, had arranged for him to travel as a 'King's Messenger'. This was an honoured position which allowed him to cross the Channel with the troops. Not long after his arrival in London, Herbert fell downstairs and damaged his knee. Sir Alfred Fripp, an eminent surgeon, recommended an immediate operation. Following his surgery, Herbert appeared to make a good recovery, but a few days later, on 2nd July 1917, he died, due to the unexpected formation of blood clots.

Iris was unable to return to England due to her husband's illness and her pregnancy. After her son Ivan was born in early 1918, they all travelled back to London, staying initially with Sybil Hart-Davis and her family in Kent. Eventually, they moved into their own flat in London, but almost immediately Curtis became ill again and spent many months in bed. Once he was fully recovered they established themselves in London's Bohemian set and became renowned for their lavish entertaining.

At around this time, Iris renewed her friendship with Nancy Cunard. However, their relationship was now tinged with jealousy as Nancy was popular with both Curtis and many of Iris' friends, particularly Sybil Hart-Davis - a situation which Iris found difficult to accept.

Ivan's upbringing was left mainly in the hands of nurses and a governess and whenever Iris wanted to escape the bonds of motherhood, she would send her son to stay with Maud. By the time he was six years old, Ivan was spending even more time with his grandmother as Iris and Curtis had virtually separated: she spent a great deal of time in Paris with Nancy Cunard, while Curtis spent most of his time away from home, having become an interior designer.

In 1925, Diana Manners (who had married Duff Cooper, brother of Sybil Hart-Davis, at the end of the war) asked Iris to perform with her in an American tour of Max Reinhardt's play *The Miracle*. Iris agreed and they set off together, much to Diana's relief as she was not looking forward to spending so much time away from her husband and knew that she could depend on her friend for companionship. Iris, despite all the temptation and enjoyment which America offered, found herself missing Ivan, so she made a speedy return, collected her son, and re-crossed the Atlantic to catch up with Diana. When the tour was almost over, Iris attended a party where she met an impoverished Austrian nobleman and aspiring actor named Friedrich Ledebur. Diana was disappointed and alarmed when Iris announced that she would not be returning to England, because she was in love with Friedrich.

Despite the protestations of Curtis, Iris and Friedrich moved in together. Friedrich earned a living as a horse trainer while waiting for his acting career to blossom. Unfortunately for Iris, this employment often involved him travelling across America, so she was frequently left alone. In the summer of 1927, Iris discovered she was pregnant. Initially friends tried to persuade her that she should terminate the pregnancy - she was, after all, still married to Curtis. At first she agreed, but at the last minute, she changed her mind and decided to have the child. She and Friedrich travelled to Europe and found lodgings in Provence. Before long, they ran out of money, so Friedrich went back to America, where there were more opportunities for him to earn a living, while Iris travelled to London. She turned to Diana Cooper for help and immediately fell in with Diana's idea that she and Duff should adopt Iris's child. Diana had longed for a child of her own for many years and this seemed like the perfect solution to everyone's problems. A plot was hatched and all the arrangements were made, but, once again, Iris changed her mind and decided that she wanted to keep her baby. Diana was understandably upset, but then found out that she was pregnant herself, so all was well.

Iris gave birth to a son on 15th February 1928 and he was named Christian, although everyone called him 'Boon'. Friedrich adopted Boon so that the child would have legal status as his son. Iris and Curtis finally divorced in 1933 and the following year she married Friedrich. The three of them lived a fairly nomadic life, travelling to wherever there was work, whether it was in Austria, California or London. Ivan, meanwhile, remained in London with his grandmother or his Aunt Viola, whose husband had died in 1933. Curtis also remarried - his new wife was Kathleen Allen, who was the opposite to Iris in both looks and character.

Every now and then Friedrich and Iris attempted to settle down in one place. For example, they moved to Ireland where Iris thoroughly enjoyed the freedom of country living and having Boon all to herself. Although their own living accommodation was fairly barren, they often went to stay at Castle MacGarret with Lord and Lady Oranmore. Friedrich was often called away on safari or to buy horses for clients, so Iris returned to writing - particularly plays. None of them were good enough to be considered for performance, but they re-ignited her interest in the stage.

She and Friedrich decided to move to Devon where they joined the Chekhov Theatre Studio. They found themselves living in a thriving community in Rednorth House and, for a while, Iris was both happy and productive. Her happiness was broken in 1937, when she received news of her mother's death. Shortly afterwards, Viola became ill and following many months in hospital, she died early in 1939.

Upon the outbreak of the Second World War, the Chekhov Studio moved to Ridgefield in Connecticut. Iris and Friedrich crossed the Atlantic with their fellow players and writers and both embarked on romantic liaisons: Friedrich with the sponsor of the theatre, and Iris with Alan Harkness, one of the teachers. When America entered the war, many students either enlisted or were drafted, so the theatre studio closed down. Iris moved to California where she was joined by Harkness and some of the other students. They converted a local school house into a theatre and started a revised version of the Studio. At around this time, Friedrich reappeared - his affair now over; Boon attended the local school and Ivan, having completed his education in England, served as an officer in the US Signal Corps.

The new theatre group was joined by actor Ford Rainey and he and Iris played the leads in Macbeth - a performance of which was attended by Charlie Chaplin and Greta Garbo. Harkness, meanwhile, married one of the female members of the group and for a while everything was settled and happy. However, having returned from a trip to Switzerland, Harkness was killed when his car was hit by a train; then Ford Rainey left to get married and so the group drifted apart. To add to Iris' woes, she received news that a former beau, Eric Meiville, had been killed in action. This report, however, turned out to be false and he and Iris met up after the war.

When the Second World War was over, Iris returned to Europe and met Duff and Diana Cooper in Paris, before travelling to London. By this time, her marriage to Friedrich was over. As ever, Iris was unable to settle in one place and moved to Rome where she frequently visited with her Uncle Max, who lived at Rapallo. Her financial position remained precarious, but on the rare occasions when she had money, she spent it on expensive face creams rather than food. She also enjoyed meeting up with old friends, such as Jenny Nicholson, the journalist daughter of Robert Graves and

Nancy Nicholson. She continued to write poetry and plays and reminisced fondly about the past.

Friedrich remarried and had another son, which Iris found difficult, unable as she was, to accept that he had managed to move on from their relationship - although they would always remain very close friends. He had become a film actor, working mainly for Federico Fellini and this work often brought him to Rome. Iris also made an appearance in a Fellini film, entitled *La Dolce Vita* and they both appeared in the 1956 version of *Moby Dick* which starred Gregory Peck. Iris's sole reason for taking on these roles was to earn money to enable her to travel more.

Boon, meanwhile, had married, had one son, divorced, remarried and had two more children. By the early 1960's he was studying medicine in Geneva. Iris went to stay in Gstaad, from where she was able to visit him and his family.

Ivan had become a successful screenwriter and sent Iris money, which enabled her to rent a house at Cadaques, a fishing port on the Costa Brava, where she became friends with Salvador Dali who lived nearby. Diana Cooper and Ivan offered to buy Iris a house in France, so she left Cadaques and arrived on the doorstep of another friend, Daphne Fielding, who lived in France. She stayed with Daphne and her husband Xan, while house-hunting. Her search proved unsuccessful, so Kathleen Moffat (widow of Curtis Moffat who had died in 1949) lent her a studio flat in Cagnes. While she was there, her car and all her papers were stolen and when a local Englishwoman called on Iris to offer her assistance, she found her extremely ill.

Iris needed immediate surgery and Boon was summoned to give his advice. He suggested that the operation would be best carried out in England. Diana Cooper made all the necessary arrangements and a few days later, Iris was in a London hospital having a large part of her colon removed. She convalesced with the Coopers, until one night when she and Diana were preparing to go to the opera together, burglars broke in, bound and gagged the two ladies, ransacked the house and made off with Diana's furs and her car. This episode had a profound effect on Iris's nerves and she felt she could no longer stay in London. She travelled to Ireland where she stayed with film director John Huston.

Once Iris had recovered, she tried to settle in London again, but found it impossible. Friedrich arranged to meet her in Paris and then drove her to the South of France, where he rented her a small villa. She had many visitors and spent hours in the local café, writing and dealing with her correspondence. Diana Cooper secretly arranged for the printing of 300 copies of her long poem *The Marsh Picnic*, with an enthusiastic introduction by John Betjeman. Iris had a wonderful surprise when she received a copy through the post. Her health, however, continued to deteriorate and she decided to move back to London, staying with Ivan and his family.

Although Iris initially continued to go out socialising, her strength waned and, as it had become clear that she was very ill, Friedrich and Boon arrived to spend some time with her. Friedrich slept on the floor of her bedroom every night, so as to be close at hand. Iris slipped into a coma on 28th April 1968, regaining consciousness just before she died to find Friedrich at her side. Her final three words were: 'Love, Love, Love', a sentiment which, throughout her tumultuous live, she had never failed to inspire.

POETRY ANALYSIS

UNTITLED POEM I -
'Of all who died in silence far away...'

This anti-war poem, essentially demonstrates the effects of death on those left behind, together with the public perception of grief and mourning at times of war. It displays many emotions which were commonly felt during the First World War, such as anger at the waste of life and the futility of the war, as well as regret for lost dreams.

The poem begins by telling us that the dead have met their end in silence a long way from home. This is said, despite the fact that war is rarely silent, because at the time of their deaths, there would have been no-one present to mourn them. In war, it seems, there is no time to sympathise because people are either busy fighting, or controlling the war, or arguing about the politics and conduct of each battle. Therefore, it seems as though the men are dying unnoticed.

Each dead soldier is perceived as small, since there are so many of them that they have almost become insignificant as individuals. This is contrasted with the greatness of the love they gave and received during their lives. While they lived, the men had control over their futures and they made plans. It is as though their hopes and dreams were like a flock of sheep and the men were shepherds, driving their lives forward, with purpose. Now, all is lost - their hopes, like them, are buried.

Looking back over their lives, Iris remembers how much the dead men were loved by their mothers who fed and cared for them. The intensity of a mother's love is so great, she says, that it is as though each mother had become the centre and focus of her son's world and he, in turn, gave her life a sense of meaning and completeness. Now, though, he has gone and she is left alone - her life is empty.

Next, our attention is drawn towards a more romantic scene of passionate young love. These young men were adored and the implication here is that many of them may have become secretly engaged before going to the front, placing a glittering jewel on the hand of their beloved. (This would not have been an unusual suggestion for Iris Tree to make as both she and her two sisters had either become secretly engaged or married). This passion has now been suppressed because the men are dead and instead of being bound to their lovers by marriage, they are bound to the earth by death.

There follows a sudden angry cry for this to stop - not just the killing, but the mourning, and the constant reminders of death. Iris goes on to tell us that those who mourn cannot always openly show their grief, possibly for fear that it will overwhelm them, but also because many, particularly in Iris's social set, were often told that they should not show their emotions, but that they should keep them hidden. The bright clothing and coloured flags represent the outward appearance which people were 'supposed' to display, while the black of mourning shows the reality which must be kept secretly locked inside, away from prying eyes. Ironically, at least one of the bright colours - a reddish orange - only serves as a reminder of spilled blood, which flows out like the train of a wedding dress and reiterates that such dreams of future contentment will remain unfulfilled.

Another outward sign of mourning would be to weep, but once again, emotions must be kept in check. The quote which follows in the poem, demonstrates the futility and waste of the war, together with the notion that the dead are somehow capable of happiness. Iris shows her view of such platitudes by reminding us that, being dead, the soldiers can neither cheer themselves, nor hear the cheering of others. She also suggests that the dead men do not understand why they died and why those they loved and left behind are not supposed to weep for them.

The first line of the last verse echoes the beginning of the poem, except that now the men have also died in darkness. This follows on from the previous verse: the darkness representing the unknown, while also introducing, for the first time, an element of fear. This emotion is only allowed a very brief acknowledgement as Iris quickly reminds us that, although the men are gone, they have left behind a wealth of love and memories. Love, she asserts, can overcome everything - even grief - so the roses on his grave are not 'blood-red', but 'passion-red', proving that love is more powerful even than death. Also, although he lies beneath the ground with his arms folded across his chest, rather than open in a loving embrace, he looks forward to a new day. It is also interesting to note the alteration in the pronoun used from 'they' and 'them', to 'his', which makes the ending of the poem even more touching and personal.

Written in 1917, this poem demonstrates the poet's anger at the waste of so many young lives and she suggests that neither those who fight, nor those who are grieving really understand what they are suffering for. This reflects her own pacifist opinions, but also demonstrates an immense depth of understanding and sympathy for both the dead and the mourning. The use of irony in this poem, particularly in the first and sixth verses, shows that she had little time for politics, rhetoric or 'socially acceptable' behaviour, when compared to human suffering.

In many ways, this poem could be compared to *When You See Millions of the Mouthless Dead* by Charles Hamilton Sorley. Both poets agree that the dead cannot speak or hear, and also that they are, to a certain extent, no longer the property of the living - they belong to death. Unlike Iris, however, Sorley suggests that to mourn is pointless, since the only people who could ever appreciate such an emotion - the dead - cannot do so, simply because they are dead. This serves to demonstrate a difference between the poetry of a non-combatant, written at a distance from the war, and that of a serving soldier. Sorley does not romanticise or sentimentalise about the war or death, or their effects on those left behind. He seems, in fact, to view death as a natural consequence of battle. Iris Tree, on the other hand, asserts that no death should go unnoticed or unmourned, and that the grieving process is a necessary means of recovering from the loss of one so beloved. Neither poet is glorifying the war - they simply view its cost from different perspectives. In Sorley's poem, the most powerful force is death. To Iris the overriding emotion, as well as the soldier's most notable legacy, is not honour, victory or sacrifice - but love.

UNTITLED POEM 2 -
'And afterwards, when honour has made good...'

This angry poem questions the validity and cost of the war, regardless of victory or defeat. It begins as though half-way through a debate, which suggests that this is a topic which is often, or even continually, being discussed, without necessarily reaching a conclusion. The poet initially asserts that even though a victory might seem desirable, honourable and just, any happiness that follows with be unfounded, since the fight itself will have proved so damaging and costly. She also questions whether those fighting really know, or remember, why they went to war, and whether, if they do, those reasons still seem justified.

When the war is over, Iris implies that the British, represented by the bulldog, will relinquish their grip on Europe and revert to their old Imperial ways. The Germans (whose national symbol, used to represent their Kings and Emperors, was the eagle) are portrayed as vanquished and fleeing the battlefields to return to their abandoned families in their devastated country. The poet could be demonstrating a sense of irony here: she may be implying that these stereotypical images of victor and vanquished will be irrelevant, since *both* sides will have ruined their countries because they will have killed off a generation of men, and also that both sides will return to their old habits - making one indistinguishable from the other, despite their proud national emblems.

Iris appears to reserve her anger most, however, for the leaders and commanders when she ironically asserts that these men should not feel any sense of shame over the course and conduct of the war. They are held up as representing the pride of the nation, which they have in fact killed, and that may explain why they seem worried and nervous. She implies that they are stained with the blood of the men for whose deaths they should be held responsible.

In the second stanza there follows a more direct series of questions as the poet asks what victory will achieve. She asks whether the old hatred between nations will be vanquished; whether such costly undertakings, bearing equally disastrous outcomes, will be a thing of the past; whether there will be any greater freedom as a result of victory. Being as these questions have an ironic tone, one may suppose that she does not expect an answer. This may be because she believes that the war will have solved nothing: there will be no answers

Maybe, she implies, the result of the war will be that the cost will prove too great: so great, in fact, that the only victors will be the gods, who will consume everything - riches, earth, power - leaving just a scent of humankind, a ritual offering of all the suffering and sorrow.

This poem was written in 1917 and is a bitter indictment of the war - its conduct, ethics and perceived outcomes. The use of questions enables the poet to demonstrate how ironic the situation is: the questions remain unanswered, partly because the war is still going on, but also because Iris does not believe that there are any answers - the end cannot justify the means. She is obviously starting to wonder whether, when it is all over, anyone will actually remember why it began. Iris also seems to believe that victory or defeat is irrelevant since no good can ever result from such evil.

The bitterness and anger of this poem, which reflects Iris's pacifist beliefs, make it reminiscent of much of Siegfried's Sassoon's poetry. Indeed Sassoon and Iris's Uncle Max met during the war, while Sassoon was on leave, and went on to form a close and lifelong friendship. Whether or not Sassoon's work had any influence on Iris is unknown as she spent almost the entire war abroad. The mood and tone of this poem, however, undoubtedly share similar traits to many of Sassoon's more bitter and satirical verses.

KATHARINE TYNAN

BIOGRAPHY

Katharine Tynan was born on January 23rd 1861 at Whitehall Dairy Farm in Clondalkin, County Dublin. Her parents, Andrew Cullen Tynan and Elizabeth Reilly Tynan had twelve children. They were a Catholic family and Andrew Tynan, as well as being a dairy farmer, was also an entrepreneur.

Katharine was educated at the Dominican Convent of St Catherine of Siena in Drogheda. Throughout her childhood, she was plagued by eye ulcers which would, in later life, lead to extreme short-sightedness. She left the convent in 1875 and immediately began writing, with her first poem being published in 1878.

In 1884, Katharine met and fell in love with Charles Gregory Fagan, an Oxford graduate and fellow poet. His untimely death the following year led her to write some very touching and emotional poetry which demonstrated her heartfelt loss.

From this time until her marriage, Katharine became a prominent member of the Celtic Revival movement which sought to reinstate traditional Irish values in literature and the arts. She became a close friend of the poet and dramatist William Butler Yeats, with whom she maintain correspondence until her death. She also frequently met Charles Stewart Parnell, the prominent Irish politician and Home Rule campaigner.

Given her Catholic upbringing and proud Irish roots, it came as quite a surprise to her family when in 1893, she married protestant writer and barrister, Henry Albert Hinkson. In fact many of her close family objected so strongly to the marriage, that Katharine was estranged from them and she and Henry moved to England. They lived in or around London until 1911. During this time, Henry struggled to earn a living at either of his professions so Katharine turned her hand to writing novels and newspaper articles to ensure they had an income.

In 1897, Katharine and Henry's first child Theobald Henry was born. Two years later, he was followed by another son, Giles Aylmer. Finally in 1900 a daughter was born. Pamela Mary Hinkson would eventually follow in her mother's footsteps, becoming a writer.

In 1911, the family returned to Claremorris, County Mayo where, two years later, Henry was appointed Resident Magistrate. This change in status and, more importantly, income enabled Katharine to devote more time to writing poetry. This was particularly so during the First World War, when the publication of her poems led her into correspondence with other anxious or bereaved families.

Both of her sons fought in the First World War. They both held the rank of Lieutenant. Theobald was in the Royal Irish Regiment, while Giles served with the Royal Dublin Fusiliers. This was an understandably difficult time for Katharine, who, together with Pamela, felt isolated in safety in the west of Ireland. They felt that the war was a remote series of events, which barely touched local lives, and yet, with Theobald and Giles both on active duty, they craved information and involvement.

Several of Katharine's friends experienced the heartbreak of losing their sons, but Katharine was lucky and both Giles and Theobald survived. Her happiness and relief were short-lived, however, when on January 11th 1919, just two months after the end of the war, Henry died suddenly at the age of 53. Katharine was devastated and the depression which had haunted her intermittently throughout her life, returned.

Eventually, Katharine rallied and she and Pamela enjoyed many visits to England and the Continent. She also continued to write both novels and poetry, until her death in Wimbledon on April 2nd 1931.

POETRY ANALYSIS

JOINING THE COLOURS

The first verse of this poem creates an image of extremely young men, marching cheerfully to war. This scene, we know from the sub-title, is taking place in the very early days of the war, yet Katharine Tynan is, unusually for that time, referring to these men as cannon-fodder. She compares the sight of them marching to a wedding procession and then reminds us that each of them, somewhere, has a mother.

In the second verse, she contrasts the happiness of these men with their dull surroundings, which implies that they are walking through the streets in a poor district of Dublin. The happiness exudes from the men rather than their surroundings; there is no flag-waving or crowds cheering them on their way. Katherine Tynan makes it clear that there are many men going, and as they pile into the trams, they sing cheerfully. They are too carefree and happy to need courage, which gives the impression that the soldiers believe they are immune to death. Yet, finally it is pointed out that they are journeying into darkness, into the unknown, or the unthinkable - to a place from which there is no return.

These soldiers do not merely sing, they use instruments too - anything which will make a noise and make their departure more celebratory, even though they are going to their deaths. Nothing can save these men - not even love. This is presumably a reference to a mother's love since the youth of the men is pointed out throughout the poem. Ordinarily, it could be assumed, that a mother would willingly sacrifice her own life to save her child, yet here, no mother can save her son.

Finally, in praising their courage and exuberance, Katharine Tynan sympathises with the young girls too. Their lives will also change when all the young men have gone. There will be no-one left for them to kiss - or, by extension, to marry. The soldiers, she claims, have appeared as through from a mist, to serve their country at this vital time; as though by magic they have materialised, yet they will disappear just as quickly, never to return.

Joining the Colours is subtitled "West Kents, Dublin, August 1914", which gives the poem an implied date. This is confirmed by the fact that The Queens Own (Royal West Kent Regiment) was in Dublin that August. It formed part of the 5th Division which helped to make up the original British Expeditionary Force which went to France in the first few days and weeks of the First World War. That this poem was written at that time, while not impossible, is unclear. The scene is that of early August 1914, the sentiment of doom and certainty of death could imply that this poem was, in fact, written retrospectively. This is not certain, however, since many people were aware of the tragic consequences of going to war before the conflict had even started, so dating this poem accurately is almost impossible.

The poem itself contains a series of mixed messages: the soldiers are happy and carefree, yet they are destined to die. In the midst of this happiness we are reminded of the things that the young men will miss - weddings, kisses, romance and the love of their mothers. Their deaths will cause great changes to those left behind: their mothers and sweethearts will suffer too. The soldiers are obviously very young and the implication throughout is that they should have had their whole lives ahead of them, but now are doomed. This mixture of feelings probably represents the poet's sensation of pride mingled with foreboding and anxiety, which was commonly felt at the beginning of the war.

The soldiers' enthusiasm to join the fight was quite usual in the early days. There existed an element of nationalist pride which, coupled with the certainty that the fighting would be all over by Christmas, encouraged young men to join up so as not to 'miss out'. In all probability it was only the mothers of these young men who fully appreciated the magnitude of their impending losses. Youth, by its very nature, gives one a sense of invulnerability or immunity to danger. There is no sense of imminent defeat - these men are marching to glorious victory.

Katharine Tynan, quite harshly, refers to the young men as foolish. Very few people were aware of what the coming four years of war would bring, or even that the war would last that long. Yet she seems almost angry with the soldiers for their lightheartedness while throwing away their lives in such a reckless fashion.

The poem also contains many repetitions of the same words used to represent youthfulness and boyhood, and the cheerful mood of the soldiers. This is done to reiterate the message of wasted youthful lives. The 'colours' of the title refer to the flags of a battalion. The King's (or Queen's) colour - for example the Union Flag; and the Regimental Colour. These, in previous wars, would have been carried into battle, but as the ways of fighting wars made this less practical, the colours were still carried around with each regiment, but not necessarily displayed. The whistles, pipes and mouths organs are noteworthy also. Music was a frequent accompaniment to military marching; but there is here also the possible implication of the ordinary soldier with his mouth organ and the officer with his whistle, piping the men into battle, as the officer's whistle was the signal for the men to go 'over the top'.

The overall tone of this poem is sadness. These happy, enthusiastic young soldiers, so keen to fight and win glory, are doomed. No mention is made of survivors, as though none are expected to live.

Nothing can save these men from their fate. The poet seems angry at the waste of life, while grateful for their courage in facing up to the challenge ahead of them.

THE BROKEN SOLDIER

The first verse creates an image of a soldier, who has been maimed and partially blinded in the war. Despite his injuries and hardships, however, he refuses to be unhappy and sings cheerfully while he works.

Next we discover that this soldier is working in the gardens at the Hall. He has been given light work to do, since he has lost one of his hands. His face is scarred, but he keeps working busily and singing while he does so.

While the soldier sings, his fellow gardeners stop their work to listen to him. They are not maimed and are more physically attractive than him, but, while they worry about insignificant things, his carefree soul shines through.

The soldier, although damaged, seems courageous and handsome because his inner being has remained untouched by his experiences. As he continues with his gardening, throughout the day, he carries on whistling and singing like a bird.

This is a poem of appreciation, tinged with sadness, but also rejoicing at the strength of human nature. The maimed soldier has obviously lost a great deal, yet has managed to remain cheerful. He also brings joy to those he works with, even though they are obviously much better off than he is. The favourable comparison between him and the other gardeners shows that his strength of character is more important than his appearance.

There is irony in the title of this poem: the soldier is physically broken, like damaged goods, he is no longer handsome, like the whole men he shares his time with, yet the description given of him makes him seem much more of a man than they are. Therefore, while he may be maimed and physically incomplete, he appears much happier than them. He has nothing to worry about, possibly because he is now safely out of the war. He may also feel grateful that he, at least, survived and one may presume, due to his injuries, that he has seen some heavy fighting, and probably the deaths of many of his comrades.

The Lady of the house, like the poet herself, obviously sympathises with the soldier, and has found him work within her grounds. This appears, in itself, to make the soldier happy. Katharine Tynan makes frequent references to birds in this poem: larks, linnets, thrushes and robins are all mentioned by name. This helps to give the impression that this soldier is as happy as these birds. The war may have broken his body, but his mind and soul remain undimmed.

This poem has a very different tone from *Joining the Colours*. Here, there is no doom, no death and no foolish hysteria. This poem has a much lighter note and, in making such a favourable comparison in the nature of the broken man compared with his whole colleagues, the poet is demonstrating her gratitude for what the soldier has sacrificed and while still remaining cheerful.

Another poem which bears some comparison with *The Broken Soldier*, is Wilfred Owen's *Disabled*. In Owen's poem, the maimed soldier, sitting in a wheelchair, regretting his past and his lost future, seems much more bitter and angry than Tynan's broken man. Owen has created a grey, dull image of the injured soldier's future, while Tynan uses nature to reflect a carefree and optimistic outlook.

However, in the very final line of *The Broken Soldier*, comes the truth: the broken soldier may be free of worries and responsibilities, but he is not free. He is trapped in a broken body, like a bird in a cage. He may sing and appear contented but he'll never fly again. The soldier's freedom has been taken from him: this has been his sacrifice. Tynan appears to be saying that he has given his freedom so that the other whole young men may be free to worry about the simple things in life. He may still be alive, but what quality of life can he expect? If he is indeed trapped like a caged bird, one's sympathy for the man and admiration of his courage, like Katharine Tynan's should be very great indeed, for what could be worse than having the capacity to understand happiness without the freedom to enjoy it?

A GIRL'S SONG

This poem begins with a description of two rivers, the Meuse and the Marne: the trees that overhang them and the green grass on their banks. There is here a reminder that the grass is given its lush colour by the bodies that lie underneath it.

In the second verse, a young French girl appears, wearing a red rose which she has picked from the ground above these graves, without acknowledging the reason for its colour. This leads us into the third stanza where the narrator asserts that the rose gains its colour from the blood of her dead lover; the yellow colour of the corn comes from his hair. However, all she has to give are tears, like the rain; and sighs, like the wind.

Next, she urges the rivers, the sheep, and even the dew to pass by her lover soundlessly, so as to not disturb his sleep. Realism creeps back into the fifth verse as she acknowledges that the earth which covers him has sealed his lips and destroyed his handsome features. She wishes she were dead too, and able to rest peacefully beside him.

In the final verse, there is recognition that spring will come again - that the earth will be reborn and life will, once again, be carefree. This realisation is tempered, however, by the fact that in making his grave look beautiful she must acknowledge the other countless dead and all must count the cost.

Judging from the title, this poem is written from the perspective of all the many young women who lost husbands or lovers. The impression given is that this poem was written after the war, or at least with a view to the end of the war, since the French girl is able to walk by the river and pick flowers, the sheep are free to roam and the narrator herself has been able to visit her lover's resting place and build a cairn.

The tone of this poem is sorrowful, demonstrating an almost overwhelming grief. The girl attributes the quality of all the beautiful things she sees - the grass, the rose, the corn - to him. Because his dead body feeds the earth, she asserts that he is responsible for the beauty that surrounds this area where he now lies. In this way, it might be said that she gives him a certain element of immortality, and also that she manages to find some justification for his death.

Although Katharine Tynan shows a clear understanding of the grief experienced by such young girls, this was not gleaned from her own sorrows. By the time the First World War started, she was in her early fifties and would have feared for the lives of her two sons, rather than a husband or lover. The rivers Marne and Meuse saw many fierce battles and their banks would have formed the final resting place for many young men, and therefore the focus of grief for many young women.

Three times during this poem, Tynan refers to the dead as sleeping, which is a rose-coloured, optimistic way of looking at death. This was fairly common amongst poets, both male and female, who, for various reasons, seem to have preferred to think of the dead as resting. For example, John McCrae's *The Anxious Dead* refers to the dead as finding true peace only once the war is won. Also May Wedderburn Cannan in *'Since They Have Died'* writes of the dead in this way. However the tone of Cannan's poem is different - she urges the living to remember the dead fondly and with smiles and states that only thus may they find true contentment. Katharine Tynan's language is just as optimistic - she dreams of spring and peace, yet the tone is more sorrowful - the grief more real.

The spring to which Tynan refers is more likely metaphorical since one is given the impression that the war has already ended, and the flowers are, once again, in bloom. Therefore the change brought by the coming of another 'spring' is more likely to be that the girl can learn to live with her grief and accept it, along with all the others who have suffered similarly.

COMPARISONS - A GUIDE

Students are frequently asked to make comparisons between poems by either the same or different poets. At first, this can seem a daunting task, but with practice it can become easier.

Obviously, the poems you will be asked to compare could be wide ranging and different and it would, therefore, be impossible for any Study Guide to provide an analysis for you. Here, however, are a few tips to help you when making comparisons.

Firstly, read both the poems through and analyse each of them as described on page nine of this Study Guide. Once you feel you have a good understanding of the poems, start to make a list of similarities and differences. Pay particular attention to themes, language and form.

If the two poems are giving opposing viewpoints, as in Jessie Pope's *Who's For The Game* and Wilfred Owen's *Dulce Et Decorum Est*, then the differences are obvious, but ask yourself are there any similarities? Do they, for example, use the same type of language?

On the other hand, the two poems may be more similar - either in content or language, so now you must look for the differences. If the language is the same, is the content different? For example, you may have two nature poems, one of which is showing the war as destructive, while the other demonstrates a more glorious viewpoint.

In making comparisons, you should always try to show differences *and* similarities. Bear in mind that the poems selected will invariably demonstrate both - your task is to discover these, illustrate your understanding and provide evidence by drawing on quotations from the text to validate and support your interpretations.

FURTHER READING

Scars Upon My Heart
Selected by Catherine Reilly
A unique and essential anthology of female poetry of the First World War, with small biographies of some of the poets.

Poems of the First World War
- Never Such Innocence
Edited by Martin Stephen
Probably one of the best anthologies of First World War poetry. Contains poems by the better known soldier-poets as well as some more obscure, or indeed, unheard of ones.

Letters from a Lost Generation: First World War Letters of Vera Brittain and Four Friends
by Vera Brittain, Alan Bishop (Editor) and Mark Bostridge (Editor)
A remarkable insight into the changes which the First World War caused to a particular set of individuals. In this instance, Vera Brittain lost four important people in her life (two close friends, her fiancé and her brother). The agony this evoked is demonstrated through letters sent between these five characters, which went on to form the basis of Vera Brittain's autobiography *Testament of Youth*.

1914-1918 Voices and Images of the Great War
by Lyn MacDonald

Like all her other books, this one is a collection of letters, diary extracts, newspaper articles and interviews, collated to form a chronological view of the real-life experiences of those who lived through the First World War. In addition, this book also contains many images and photographs, which help bring this era to life.

Siegfried Sassoon - The Making of a War Poet:
A Biography 1886-1918
and
Siegfried Sassoon - The Journey from the Trenches:
A Biography 1918-1967
both by Jean Moorcroft Wilson

These two books form a definitive biography of Siegfried Sassoon and, in particular, prove useful in providing an insight into the relationships formed between poets and writers before, during and after the First World War.

These books and others may be purchased through our Web site bookstore at: www.greatwarliterature.co.uk/bookstore.html

BIBLIOGRAPHY

Grey Ghosts and Voices
by May Wedderburn Cannan

Scars Upon My Heart
Edited by Catherine Reilly

1914-1918: Voices and Images of the Great War
by Lyn MacDonald

**Siegfried Sassoon - The Journey from the Trenches:
A Biography 1918-1967**
by Jean Moorcroft Wilson

**Poems of the First World War
- Never Such Innocence**
by Martin Stephen

The Rainbow Picnic - A Portrait of Iris Tree
by Daphne Fielding

Eleanor: Portrait of a Farjeon
by Denys Blakelock

Portrait of a Family
by Eleanor Farjeon

www.spartacus.schoolnet.co.uk

www.modjourn.brown.edu

The Edith Nesbit Society Web Site

OTHER GREAT WAR LITERATURE STUDY GUIDE TITLES

Paperback Books

Birdsong	ISBN 1905378238
Journey's End	ISBN 1905378165
Regeneration	ISBN 190537822X
Strange Meeting	ISBN 1905378211
War Poets of the First World War - Volume One	ISBN 1905378246

Great War Literature Study Guide E-Books (Electronic Books) on:

Novels & Plays

Birdsong	ISBN 1905378181
Journey's End	ISBN 1905378173
Regeneration	ISBN 190537819X
Strange Meeting	ISBN 1905378203

Poets

Rupert Brooke	ISBN 1905378033
Female War Poets 1: WM Letts; M Postgate Cole; E Nesbit	ISBN 1905378114
Female War Poets 2: MW Cannan; K Tynan; C Mew	ISBN 1905378327
Wilfrid Wilson Gibson	ISBN 1905378149
Julian Grenfell	ISBN 1905378084
E A Mackintosh	ISBN 1905378335
John McCrae	ISBN 1905378157
Robert Nichols	ISBN 1905378025
Wilfred Owen	ISBN 1905378017
Jessie Pope	ISBN 1905378106
Isaac Rosenberg	ISBN 1905378130
Siegfried Sassoon	ISBN 1905378041
Charles Hamilton Sorley	ISBN 1905378092
Edward Thomas	ISBN 1905378122